SIR H. NORMAN RAE
1860 - 1928

Our Local Benefactor

G. SHUTTLEWORTH
and
M. WALKER

First published in 2000 by
Moorhead Press
31 Moorhead Crescent, Shipley

Printing by FM Repro Ltd.
69 Lumb Lane, Roberttown, Liversedge, West Yorkshire WF15 7NB
Tel: (01924) 411011   Fax: (01924) 411196

ISBN 0-9538224-0-0

This book is dedicated to the late Lady Emily Rae,
who played a vital but unrecorded role in this story.

CONTENTS

Page

Sir Henry Norman Rae. Biography

Preface

Henry Norman Rae was born in 1860, the third son of the Rev. and Mrs. James Rae of Batley. He chose as his career, not the Ministry like his father nor the manufacturing and drapery business of his Scottish forbears, but the thriving woollen trade of the West Riding of Yorkshire.

Apprenticed at the age of fourteen to a highly respected wool buyer, Abraham Brooke, Norman quickly gained the knowledge and experience which was to enable him, eventually, to become a very wealthy man. However, he did not confine his activities solely to his business, becoming elected as the Member of Parliament for the Constituency of Shipley for the years 1918 - 1923, when he resigned from his Parliamentary duties. His world wide knowledge of the woollen industry enabled him to be of great service, in an advisory capacity, to the Government, (he was knighted in 1922).

Throughout all his adult life he strove to improve the qualitity of life for his fellow men, especially in his Constituency. His wealth enabled him to purchase the large area of land at Shipley which he presented to the Council for the enjoyment and recreation of the public, forever. He took a great interest in the welfare and higher education of boys and girls, encouraging University entrants by the gift of scholarships. He bought and established a Nursing Home where many generations of children were born in up-to-date facilities. The Northcliffe Golf Club, which was founded on land which he bought and gave, has given pleasure to many, country wide. Oakwell Hall, an Elizabethan house at Birstall, was saved from being sold and perhaps transported to America by the timely intervention of himself and his friend, John Sharman.

On his death in 1928, it was reported in the Shipley Council minutes that "Sir Norman was the greatest benefactor to the Shipley District since the time of the late Sir Titus Salt".

Yet in Shipley, there is no recognition or reference to him beyond a plaque on the main gates to the playing fields, originally designated. "The Norman Rae Playing Fields" and now spoken of as Northcliffe Park, and a framed photograph of him in Northcliffe Golf Club. Todays generation need ask "Who was Norman Rae?"

This small book is intended to answer that question. It cannot be a full answer, too long a time has passed and with time have gone the friends who would have been all too pleased to fill the gaps of the story, but in a small way the book should prove enlightening to the question, "Who was Sir Norman Rae?"

GS. MW. 2000.

FOREWORD
By Councillor Tony Miller
(Lord Mayor of Bradford 1998-99)

It gives me great pleasure to add a foreword to this fascinating book charting the life and works of Sir Henry Norman Rae, MP.

One of my fondest memories from my year as Lord Mayor of Bradford was being called upon to officially receive the Golden Key for the Northcliffe Estate from the Friends of Northcliffe. The Friends made the presentation on behalf of Sir Norman's grand-daughter, Mrs. Hofer, to whom the key had originally been presented as a memento by Shipley Council, back in June 1920, at the age of 7. That ceremonial key now takes pride of place in Shipley Town Hall, as a permanent reminder of one of Shipley's greatest philanthropists and I like to think that that would have pleased Sir Norman. Mrs. Hofer, who sadly died shortly after the presentation took place, was certainly delighted that the key — and with it the memories of that summer day some 79 years earlier — were honoured in that way.

Living, as we do, in an age much concerned with materialism and self-interest, it is both timely and instructive to reflect upon the guiding sentiments which shaped the lives of people like Sir Norman Rae. At the official opening of Northcliffe Woods and Playing Fields Sir Norman said, "The amassing of gold, merely for the love of gold, is a sorry business. By the use we make of our opportunities, whether by deed or gift, we shall be judged". The Council has respected his heartfelt and altruistic desire that the Northcliffe Estate should be preserved and improved upon for the benefit of the people of Shipley. This wonderful book, which sheds light upon his life and deeds, in no small way adds to the legacy of one of Shipley's finest benefactors. That his memory and works live on in this way is as fitting a tribute as one could wish to make.

Councillor Tony Miller
Lord Mayor of Bradford, 1998-99

INTRODUCTION

In 1990, a group of people came together to help to preserve the lovely woods and fields of Northcliffe for future generations. Calling themselves the "Friends of Northcliffe" they formed a good relationship with Bradford Metropolitan Council. Under the guidance of the Woodlands Manager, Richard Dunton, and the Recreation Manager, Malcolm Wright, they have achieved many worthwhile projects.

In 1995 it was decided to hold a Gala event on the meadow in Northcliffe Woods to mark the 75th. anniversary of the gift of Northcliffe to the people of Shipley by Sir Henry Norman Rae. One of the "Friends", Margaret Walker, had done a great deal of research in various archives and libraries, collecting much interesting information on the life of Sir H. Norman Rae. He died in 1928 so now there are few people who can remember him, but the older generation could remember being told about him by their parents. He was always described as being a "good" man, and having done more for Shipley than any other man before or since.

When Margaret's collected data was put on display on the Gala day it aroused much interest, many younger people saying that, though they had heard his name mentioned, they knew nothing more about him. Reading through those photo-copies of the old newspapers, I found that I did not know much either! It seemed to be a sensible project to find and record more about this generous benefactor before he was forgotten altogether.

Margaret began a more diligent search through the archives of West Yorkshire, and I began to thread together the story of the life of this remarkable man. As it evolved, it became apparent that he was born and bred the man he was, eventually, to become. He was a man of his time, but shaped by his ancestry to be one of the best of his time.

I never knew him, but my father spoke well of him, saying one day when we were walking in Northcliffe, "Remember, Norman Rae gave us these woods, you must always say 'Thank You'", which, as a child, I duly promised to do.

So, with Margaret's help, and some seventy - odd years later, this book is my "Thank You" to Sir Henry Norman Rae, M.P.

G.Shuttleworth. 2000.

Coming from my home town of Knaresborough, I had no reason to have heard about Sir Norman Rae. It was not until I joined the Friends of Northcliffe that I realized he had done so much for Shipley.

For the Thanksgiving Gala I was delegated to do the research on his gifts, which at the time I did not realize extended beyond Shipley. After the Gala, Gladys and I decided to team up and produce a booklet for general information. The "booklet" developed into this book!

We had the pleasure of meeting Sir Norman's grandson, Mr. Norman Woodhead and Mrs. Woodhead when they attended the re-opening of Shipley Hospital in 1996. Mr. Woodhead and his sister, the late Mrs. Hofer, provided us with family photographs which otherwise would have been unavailable.

I am very grateful for the help I have been given in gaining the necessary information required for the basis of this book. I would also like to include in my thanks the many people I have met, both personally and over the phone.

Margaret Walker.

ACKNOWLEDGEMENTS

Our thanks to all the people who have encouraged and assisted us in recording as much as possible of the life of Sir Henry Norman Rae.

To his grandson and grand-daughter, Mr. Norman Woodhead and the late Mrs. Marion Jean Hofer, for advice and photographs of the opening of the Norman Rae Nursing Home and Northcliffe Woods; the portraits of their grandfather, and much valuable memorabilia.

To all the Librarians of the libraries listed for sharing their expertise and time in tracking down elusive reports.

To Mr. Stuart Main, Baildon Historian, for his advice on printing and publishing.

Our thanks to Mrs. Linda Horne for patiently converting our word-processor disc.

To all the un-named journalists whose careful recording of events from 1860 - 1928. have proved invaluable. Without all these people this book would never have been written.

GS. and MW.

H. N. Rae, as a young man. Studio portrait taken in Australia.

CHAPTER ONE

Roots and Shoots

In the "Dictionary of British Surnames" (P.H. Reaney) the surname Rae is described as the Scottish form of Roe. There was a Robert Rae c. 1231 and an earlier date of 1170, William Le Roo.

The branch of the family which is of our interest, was, in the early 18th. century, at Lumphanan, a small hamlet in Deeside. Its very name is said to mean, "bare little village". It was here that Macduff was reputed to have killed Macbeth in 1057, the spot being marked by a cairn (Peel of Lumphanan, a famous medieval earthwork castle). The parish church dates from 1762, the year before John Rae (Sir Norman's great-grandfather) was born. It was from this village that, as a young hand-loom weaver, he travelled some forty miles south to Laurencekirk, Kincardineshire.

Built in the local dull-red sandstone, Laurencekirk is situated in the district known as "Howe o' the Mearns". An account in 1755 gives the population of the parish as 757, varying little from the beginning of the century. Most of the inhabitants were dependent on agriculture for their livelihood. Life was harsh as they had little protection from the vagaries of the weather and farmers faced ruin after successive poor harvests. Farm implements were still very primitive in design, not even the simple farm cart had come into general use.

The defeat of Prince Charles at Culloden was still within living memory but the Jacobite risings had subsided.

Scotland was slowly emerging from over a century of religious and political struggle. Lowland law was applied to Highland tenures; chiefs became landlords, their faithful followers became their tenants, but not for long. Brutality and inhumanity in one form or another seemed inescapable; the infamous clearances of crofters and tenants, their land required for the more profitable business of sheep rearing, is still to this day a dark period in Scottish history.

But Laurencekirk had a mentor, Lord Gardenstone, an advocate and proprietor of the estate of Johnstone. Before he became a peer, Francis Garden was a lawyer practising in Edinburgh. It was considered expedient and profitable at that time to invest in the purchase of land, preferably a small village or town with potential for development. Those who realised this ambition also regarded it a duty to take a paternalistic as well as an economic self - interest in their property and tenants. In 1779 Lord Gardenstone addressed his tenants at Laurencekirk saying, "The relationship of master and tenant, like Prince and people, implies a reciprocal duty and mutual affection, beneficence to the tenants is the best privilege of landed property".

He put his views into practice by encouraging settlers to the community and by giving aid, if needed, to help establish the trade of hand - loom weaving. The linen produced was of such high quality that it was supplied to the Royal Households. The snuffboxes made by a Laurencekirk craftsman, Charles Stiven, were greatly sought after, and are highly collectable today. He had devised an ingenious concealed hinge and pin in his fine work. Lord Gardenstone's whole outlook was one of support and advancement, favouring local industry and independence. In 1779 he obtained the town's promotion to a burgh of barony, i.e. "a borough having a charter from the sovereign but holding its land from a feudal lord."

In this encouraging atmosphere John Rae became a master draper and manufacturer and, having married Anne Molyson on the 15th. November 1794, in due course became the father of three children. The eldest son, John, was born in 1796, then James in 1797 and Anne in 1800. As one of the original feuars in the burgh, his was one of the twenty - one portraits painted by the Dutch artist, Brich, who had been commissioned by Lord Gardenstone at a salary of £20 a year. (The portraits hung in the Gardenstone Arms for many years but are now thought to have been destroyed).

Laurencekirk was becoming more widely known in other ways than industry. It is reputed that Dr. Johnson called to see the library, which had been installed in the Gardenstone Arms by Lord Gardenstone, and the town council was one of the first to approve a Sunday School for children. But times were hard and wages were low. A poignant inscription on a house wall in Gardenstone Street reads :-

1814.   We thought of better times.
1816.   But worse came.

When John Rae died in 1845 his business was transferred to his eldest son, John, both father and son being described as exemplary citizens.

John Rae the second was twice married, first to Catherine Dunbar in 1821. They had six children, Anne

3

born 1823, James 1825, Jessie 1828, John 1830, David 1834 and Catherine 1838. After the death of his first wife, John married Isabella Milne and they had one daughter, Isabella Jane, born 1858. The census for 1851 gives his address as 15, Johnston Street, Laurencekirk. The building of this street was, in 1820, known as the new town. He died in 1877.

Lord Gardenstone had died in 1793, but not before he had given the town its first council. He made proposals on how it should conduct its affairs, reminding the officers that it was not in their power to sanction embezzlement of funds or eat or drink them as done in other burghs in Scotland. On the whole it would be fair to say that the people of Laurencekirk were law - abiding and God - fearing citizens. There was still a Calvinistic influence in religion in Scotland which coloured their daily life, but in 1843 the Evangelicals broke away from the Church of Scotland; about four hundred ministers left to form the Free Church. Congregational services were held for a while in the Town Hall at Laurencekirk until 16th. October 1842 when their own chapel was opened for public worship.

John Rae the third married Elizabeth Duncan at Inverbervie in 1858, and they had four children, Helen Mary, James, Alfred and Elizabeth. He was elected Bailie in 1876, the third holder of the name which had been on the list of burghesses from the beginning. His great, great grandson is in possession of an illuminated address dated 1892, presented to John Rae in appreciation from the grateful burghesses. There is a photograph of him in the possession of his relative, Mr James Rae of Laurencekirk.

But it is to John Rae's elder brother, James, that we turn our attention. He was to become the father of Henry Norman, the future Member of Parliament for Shipley. James trained for the ministry at Cheshunt College, Herts, and obtained his degree at London University. He began his ministerial duties first at Listerhills Congregational Chapel, Bradford in 1854 (having come to the West Riding because the ministerial needs were greater in an area of rapid industrial and population growth). In the same year he was married, at the College Chapel, Cheshunt, to Elizabeth Dewey, whose family farmed in the area. He was soon to become pastor at the Batley Congregational Chapel, living with his wife at Healey until a new chapel and manse were built in 1868 at Hanover Street, Batley. Described as a "highly ornamental building in the Gothic style of architecture", it had large and convenient adjoining schools which altogether gave it a college-like appearance.

The new minister and his wife were a popular young couple. In addition to the Bible classes the Rev. Rae gave great help to his students in English literature and elementary science. His wife often deputised for him if he was detained in other duties. Under his wise ministry the affairs of the Chapel prospered and there was an encouraging increase in the attendance. In addition to his parochial duties, he found time to be secretary of the West Riding Provident Society, a benevolent institution for the relief by annuity of aged or infirm ministers and their families. He was a trustee of both Pateley Bridge and Batley District cottage hospitals and lent his support to Silcoates School, which was a Congregational establishment near Wakefield. He was on the school council for many years as a school governor. James and Elizabeth had six children, Charles James born 1856, William Dunbar 1858, Henry Norman 1860, Alice Edith, Clunie Katherine, and Lucy Susanna the youngest, 1870.

At this time, Batley was developing into a town of some importance in the manufacture of shoddy, a form of spinning and weaving which blends old woollen-cloth fibres with new, giving a cheaper but durable material. This invention brought a wave of prosperity to Batley and its people. As with all fast growing towns, it was at some cost of the lovely countryside surrounding the old parts of the town. People mourned the loss of the pleasant woods and watched the once clear streams become black with waste from the mills, but there was the compensation of good roads, better housing and full employment at the mills. There must have been an air of prosperity and stability for the children growing up in the manse in Hanover Street.

They were a happy and lively young family, three boys and three girls, with wise and loving parents. Perhaps there was many a tale told of the grandparents and uncles in Laurencekirk, of how Lord Gardenstone devoted his time, money and energy to the further promotion of the town and its peoples. An example of true co-operation between man and master, one which would have made a deep and lasting impression on the boys in particular. There was good company too amongst the members of the congregation at their father's Church, Mr. A. Brooke and some of the members of the Taylor family were to have closer connection and influence in later years. This, and their parents' unstinting support must have made for a very secure childhood. Their father's quiet advice, "You can

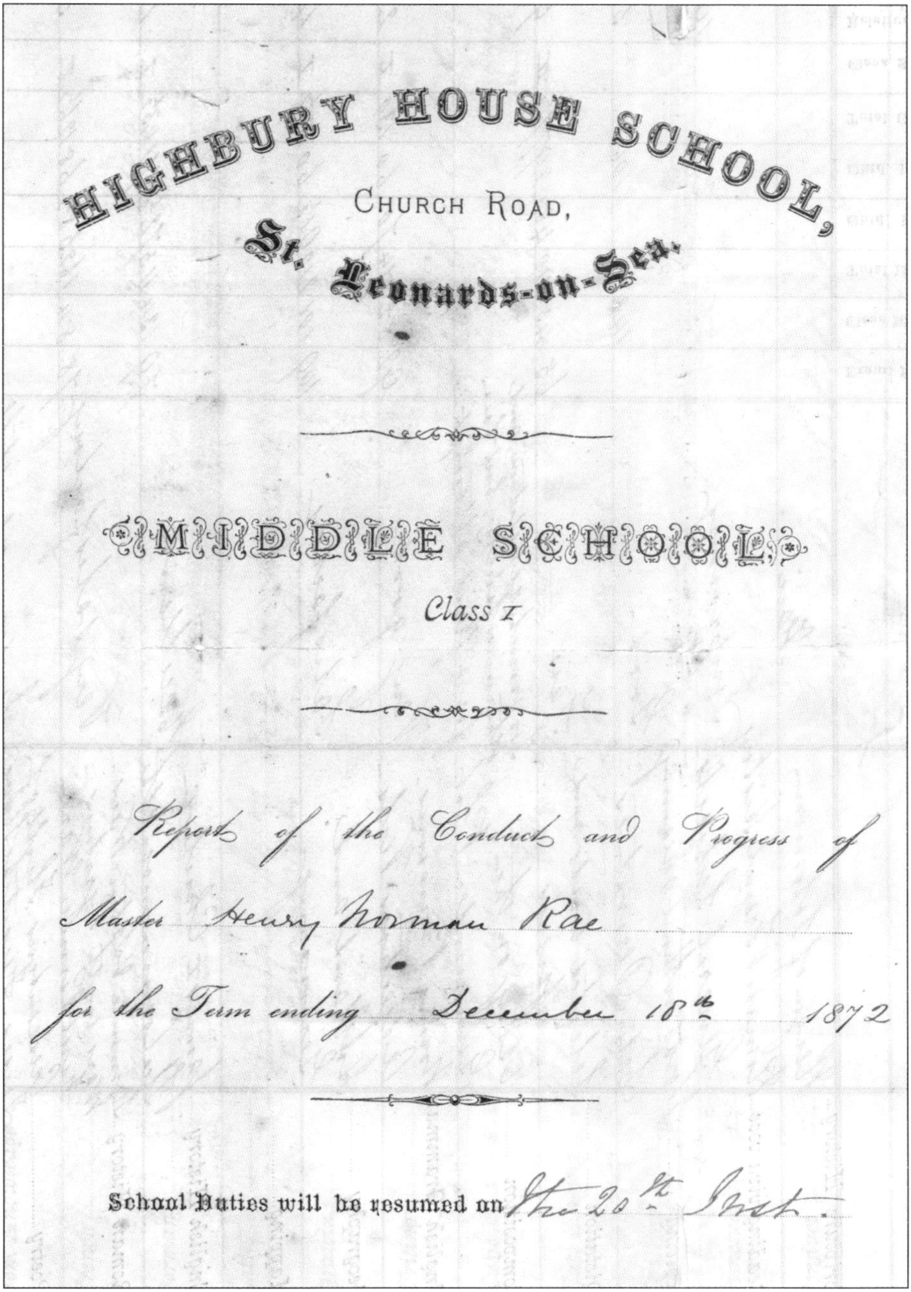

HIGHBURY HOUSE SCHOOL,

CHURCH ROAD,

St. Leonards-on-Sea.

MIDDLE SCHOOL,

Class I

Report of the Conduct and Progress of

Master Henry Norman Rae

for the Term ending December 18th 1872

School Duties will be resumed on the 20th Inst.

School Report.

Highbury House.
St. Leonards-on-Sea.
October 31st. 1873.

My dear Mamma

Mr. Wooding gave us
an half-holiday on Monday
because we had not been able
to get out for a game of football for some few days owing
to the bad weather. It has
begun to be very cold and we
have put on our flannels. Mrs.
Duff has finished Barnaby
Rudge and is now reading
Silas Marner which is a much
quieter book than Barnaby
Rudge. On Sundays she is
reading Martin Luther and
has got to where he goes into the
convent. It was Hastings regatta
on Monday but we did not go
to see it as Mr. Wooding said
we were not to. I received a letter
from Alice, week before last and
she and Edith were very well

Mrs. Duff has given me a new Sunday
cap and said my other one was to be used for
our walks. With best love to all, from,
    Your loving son
        Norman.

Letter to mother, 1873.

give up when you have done!" shows a development of tenacity and patience, there must have been many a youthful sigh before "done" was declared!

Batley Grammar School provided the education of early years for the boys. Later Charles went to Silcoates, the school his father helped to support (as an old boy, Charles was the organiser of a fund to provide a new swimming bath for the school). In 1873 Norman was at Highbury House, St. Leonards-on-Sea, from where he wrote to his mother a dutiful letter in beautiful copperplate handwriting, describing the English literature reading of "Barnaby Rudge" and "Silas Marner". Also that the weather had turned cold, it was October 31st, and "We have put on our flannels and could not go to Hastings regatta as Mr.Wooding said we were not to". There is an air of loneliness about the letter, the weather had been too bad for a game of football - he was thirteen years old. His school report for the previous year shows him to have excellent marks for English history with only "very fair" for the lovely handwriting! In the Batley Grammar School Magazine of a much later date, mention is made of Norman's attendance at Silcoates prior to entering his apprenticeship with Abraham Brooke in 1874.

Norman must have chosen apprenticeship instead of University. Abraham Brooke was a wool merchant of Batley. A wealthy man, he lived at Croft House, Soothill, and was a deacon and member of Hanover Congregational Church, a man known for his scrupulous honesty in all his dealings. Norman began his career as a buyer in the wool trade, a job with many facets; travel, meeting people and the delicate task of making shrewd and honest purchases.

132 Piccadilly. London
Mar 12.78.

Dear Sir,

I find a letter of yours dated Feby 8th which has not been answered & which it is not easy to answer.

In regard to public speaking, the first thing required is that you should thoroughly understand the question you are to speak upon, & know what you wish to impress upon your audience - then you should speak in a clear manner so that your meaning may be clearly understood - You should not seek to say all that may or might be said, but only as much as may be reasonably expected to convince, - & you should speak with an honest desire to be truthful & to serve only

what is true. & you should make no effort merely for display - for nothing is less pleasing than an exhibition of vanity & arrogance in a public speaker.

It is a good thing to use few words & the best words - which are those which are simple & forcible - with no needless use of adjectives, too many of which spoil speaking & writing.

To assist in attaining to a practice like this. the reading of good books, I mean, well written books is helpful, so that the eye & the ear, & the mind may become familiar with good language.

Practice in speaking is of course, of great use - & it is well always to study to do the best - to be simple, clear, truthful & earnest, & brief as the case may admit of it.

To some, public speaking will come easily - to some it may never come, or come imperfectly & with great difficulty. Nature in many things has set bounds which we may not pass over. Of your case I know nothing - but I may urge you not to aspire to speak out of vanity & for display - If you have any natural gift, cultivate & cherish it, but always & only

for good & for truth. & the love of what is true will help to give you strength.

I am afraid this will not be of much service to you - but I write it just as it comes to my mind & my pen, as I attempt to hastily reply to your letter which I have neglected for a month or more.

I hope when you speak, you will always strive to speak for what you believe to be right.

I am respy yours
John Bright

W.H.N. Rae
Hanover St
Batley

Letter from John Bright M.P., 1878.

He progressed well and in 1878 was obviously thinking beyond his current position. He wrote to John Bright, Quaker and Parliamentarian, asking his advice on the art of public speaking. Bright's reply was one that the eighteen-year-old boy was to treasure all his life. The letter still exists and it seems appropriate to quote it here in full.

132. Piccadilly.

London.

12. 3.1878.

Dear Sir,

I find a letter of yours dated Feb. 8th. which has not been answered and which it is not easy to answer.

In regard to public speaking, the first thing required is that you should thoroughly understand the question you are to speak upon and know what you wish to impress upon your audience. You should then speak in a clear manner so that your meaning may be clearly understood. You should not wish to say all that may or might be said, but only as much as may be reasonably expected to convince. You should speak with an honest desire to be truthful and to serve what is true and you should make no effort merely for display - for nothing is less pleasing than an exhibition of vanity and arrogance in a public speaker.

It is a good thing to use a few words and the best words - which are those which are simple and forcible - with no needless use of adjectives, too many of which spoil public speaking and writing.

To assist in attaining to a practice like this, the reading of good books, I mean well-written books, is helpful, so that the eye and the ear and the mind may become familiar with good language.

Practice in speaking is of course of great use, and it is wise always to study to do the best - to be simple, clear, truthful, in earnest and brief as the case may admit of it.

To some, public speaking will come easily - to some it may never come, or come imperfectly and with great difficulty. Nature in many things has set bounds, which it may not pass over. Of your case I know nothing - but may I urge you not to aspire to speak out of vanity and for display. If you have any natural gift, cultivate it and cherish it, but always and only for good and for truth, and the love of what is true will help to give you strength.

I am afraid this will not be of much service to you, but I write it just as it comes to my mind and my pen, as I attempt a hasty reply to your letter which I have neglected for a month or more.

I hope that when you speak, you will always strive to speak for what you believe to be right.

I am resp. Yours,

John Bright.

Mr.H.N.Rae.
Hanover Street.
Batley.

The wise words and high standards of the veteran speaker, John Bright, might have seemed almost unattainable to the young man, but they stayed with him like a bright beacon in all the years to come. (It is interesting to note that a Batley street was named after John Bright).

Norman's employer, Mr. Abraham Brooke, later to become the senior partner of Messrs. A. Brooke and Co., had himself served an apprenticeship to the wool trade in the mill of Mr. Watson of Soothill. In "Batley - Past and Present" by James Willans, Abraham Brooke is described as "One of the largest buyers at the London wool sales, no doubt upright fair dealing, along with a knowledge of the business, has been the means of securing so large a circle of customers". Mr. Brooke's house is described as "Surrounded by pleasant hedges of elder and thorn. Not far away stood a wood at the side of Greenhill Beck in whose waters roach swam and long-tailed tits nested in the hedge-rows". There were "selling houses" and warehouses in Station Road. but it is not certain which "selling house" belonged to Mr. Brooke. The name "Greenhill" recurs throughout Norman's career, so much so that it must have held special memories. Did the three brothers fish in the clear waters of beck?

CHAPTER TWO

A public man

Norman worked hard and learned well. He was a competent organist and his love of music led him to join the choir at his father's church. There he met and fell in love with a young lady, Miss Emily Cass of Carlinghow, who was becoming well known as a solo contralto. Norman was charmed by her singing and personality. They were married at Batley Independent Church on July 30th. 1883, the Rev. James Rae officiating. The newly-weds' first home was at Cross Park Street, Batley, where their daughter, Cassie, was born in 1886. Later they moved to 3, Cleveland Road, North Park Road, Bradford, where their son, Norman Dunbar was born.

During this period Abraham Brooke had ceased trading and Norman was working successfully on his own account. The West Riding of Yorkshire was acknowledged as the centre of the woollen industry. World markets were opening to the great mills which had grown apace, but as demands for goods grew, competition became fiercer. German and Continental manufacturers vied for the lucrative export trade to the Far East, but there was a steadily growing market for British firms in the colonies of Canada and Australia. Merino wool from Australia boosted the worsted production but fashion is fickle and demand for fine cloth waxed and waned. Softer dress fabrics were in vogue and the style of ladies garments altered to suit the newer materials. Fortunes were made and lost as manufacturers and designers fought for the markets against foreign competition and the severity of foreign tariffs on

British goods. There is a familiar ring to one man's complaint ;-

"Really! the intricacies of the tariff make one feel that it was put together, not only to protect the French manufacturer, but to raise so many difficulties for the foreigner as to make him disgusted with the whole".

The latter years of Queen Victoria's reign were ones of steady prosperity for England, and boom years for the West Riding of Yorkshire. With the high demand for woollen goods came the increased need for supplies of coal and machinery. Trade to the Far East soared. It is a sad fact that war and misfortune in one part of the world can mean improved trade and prosperity in another. Reporting on the Russo - Japanese war, 1904-5, a Dewsbury newspaper observed - "It's an ill wind that blows nobody good. The war in the Far East is deplorable but has brought the district good fortune.... one firm in this neighbourhood is engaged on a contract for no fewer than 800,000 blankets for the Japanese army, two others at Earlsheaton are turning out 101,000 and a Batley Carr house is providing 60,000".

Busy as Norman was, travelling widely, and progressively establishing his business, he still found time to help and advise whenever his wide experience could be of benefit. He had already served on the board of Batley Education Committee. Like his father he maintained a keen interest in educational affairs. Possibly from his mother and his maternal grandparents came his involvement and interest in agricultural problems. In 1902 he led, at his own expense, a party of Yorkshire farmers to

Letterhead, "Pickles and Rae".

Rossett Green
Harrogate
Dec 23. 1910

Now our fight is over I want to
tell you how I appreciate the work
you did for me during our
campaign – Never had candi-
-date more loyal workers. If
hard earnest labour could have
brought success, surely victory
would have been ours. You & I
gave of our best, we succeeded in
materially reducing the majority
against us, few County Divisions
have done this. Once more let
me thank you for your untiring
labours in our cause,
    Mrs Rae & myself wish you a
pleasant Christmas & Happy New Year,
    Yours very truly,
        H Norman Rae

Christmas card thanking friend for Election support, Ripon 1910.

Denmark to enable them to study the dairying methods of that country. In later years he expressed his regret that British agriculture had not taken more note and put into practice these productive ideas.

In 1904 he was elected to the West Riding County Council as a representative of the Pateley Bridge electoral division, on which he served for the next nine years. He was also the first chairman of the Smallholdings Committee for the same Council. Eventually, he went into partnership with a Mr.William Pickles. As woolcombers and top makers at 13, Union Street, Bradford, they traded as Pickles and Rae. The partnership was a very successful one and in 1907 they acquired Greenhill Mills, Florence Street, Laisterdyke. They re-built much of the mill and doubled its capacity. It was in this year that the wool exports reached their highest level for over thirty years.

By this time the family had moved to "Fairlea", 19, Beech Grove, Harrogate; a pleasant place, convenient for access to both Pateley Bridge and Bradford. These years were an intensively busy period in Norman's career. Due to his high degree of acumen in management and knowledge of wool, the firm of Pickles and Rae was eminently successful, with offices in Melbourne, Sydney, Adelaide and Brisbane. He had spent much time in Australia, even acquiring an estate, Greenhill Farm (of which his nephew, Leonard, was later appointed manager).

As well as travelling, often accompanied by his wife, Norman retained his close ties with Pateley Bridge and the Ripon Parliamentary Division. A popular councillor and friend of the Dales people, he generously provided, with the agreement of the Yorke family of Bewerley, a handsome pavilion to be erected in the riverside park at Pateley Bridge. His father, the Rev. James Rae, had a long association with both the hospital at Pateley Bridge and the one at Batley. The name of Rae was well known and respected. Norman, always a staunch Liberal and a supporter of Free Trade, was however, unsuccessful as candidate in the Ripon Division of the 1910 Parliamentary Election. The Hon. Edward Wood, Conservative. gained the seat.

1910 was a momentous year in Parliament. The Liberals were intent upon curtailing the powers of the Lords whose Members wished to preserve their powers intact. A Bill had been introduced in April of that year, but then there followed the death of Edward VII and the accession of George V. It was a very controversial Bill and both the Commons and the Lords were anxious to avoid the embarrassment of a major disagreement to the new King. Asquith, the Liberal Prime Minister, obtained a promise from George V. to create sufficient new Liberal Peers to pass the Bill, if the Lords persisted and forced another general election. It was this election of December 1910 which Norman Rae had unsuccessfully contested. A copy of his electoral speech exists and it is worth quoting here in full. It illustrates the unfairness of the Parliamentary system prevalent at the time.

Electors of the Ripon Division.

An election is about to take place, at which you will be asked to decide a momentous question. That question is : **"WHO ARE TO RULE, THE PEOPLE OR THE PEERS?"** All has been done that friendly, candid discussion by Conference can do. There is nothing left now but to fight it out at the polls. Where do we stand? The Peers have the last word. If they veto a Bill, the Bill is dead.

What is their record in the last 15 years :

1895-1905 - (Ten Tory years)

NOT A SINGLE GOVERNMENT BILL VETOED.

1905-1910 - (Five Liberal years)

11 GOVERNMENT BILLS VETOED AND 7 MUTILATED.

This shows clearly that the House of Peers vetoes only Liberal Bills, and is little less than Tory caucus.

I am in favour of a second chamber, but it must be one that treats all parties with equal fairness. The Government Bill ensures this. It provides for revision and delay, but leaves the last word with the PEOPLE'S HOUSE OF COMMONS.

The Peers arrogate to themselves rights they deny to you and me - rights of birth not of merit. We are Englishmen as they are. We love our country as they do. We pay taxes as they do.

The Peers say in effect all classes may have votes but only Tory votes are to count. We say this injustice must cease. We claim equal rights, and are determined to have them.

I am a Free Trader. Our export of manufactures is over one million sterling for every working day in the year. Protection must increase the cost of production, and so

Family photograph
Left to right- H. N. Rae, daughter Cassie aged 11, Emily Rae (nee Cass), son
Norman aged 3 and Ada aged 18, adopted daughter, niece of Mrs Rae.

seriously imperil this vast trade without which we, as a nation, cannot exist. Let us leave well alone.

My wish to be of service to the agricultural interest is well - known. I come of farming stock. All proposals for the benefit of farmers, consistent with the general good of the nation, will be supported by me without regard to Party. Inspectors of the Board of Agriculture should be practical farmers and not retired Army officers.

I will do my best to visit every part of the Division, and lay my views before you on other questions.

Yours faithfully,

H. NORMAN RAE.

At the time of writing this, the Rae family had moved to Rossett Green, Harrogate, a very desirable area in which to live. Norman Rae was now an established and well respected businessman. Travelling widely in search of new markets in South America, the United States, New Zealand and Australia, Norman managed to avoid much unemployment for his workforce. There existed a happy relationship with his employees at Greenhill Mills. For many years a bonus scheme, which he had introduced, had been in operation. This was much appreciated by the workpeople.

When war was declared in 1914 he made an arrangement for all the men who were called up or volunteered. A fund was set aside to make good the difference between their army pay and what their earnings would have been at the mill. There was also a promise to re-instate all employees when hostilities ceased. This must have been a great consolation to the men at the front, knowing that their families could truly "Keep the home fires burning".

He had not, however, abandoned his aim of being elected to Parliament, and at the 'khaki' election of 1918, the Liberals selected him as their Coalition Candidate for the Shipley Division. Norman Rae had supported the need for coalition. In his Election speech he expressed an opinion that "The best elements of all parties should still combine for a solution of the immense problems with which we are faced". One of these problems, the solution of which was held in deep and true belief by him, was that of the need for good education, especially Higher Education, which would lead to University entrance.

In many cities it was decided by the authorities that a fitting memorial to the young men who had lost their lives in the conflict would be the establishment of scholarships. In Bradford, the City Council set up a fund to provide the opportunity of Higher Education for its young men and women. Prominent amongst the benefactors were the names of Titus Salt, Isaac Holden, the Mitchell Brothers, and Norman Rae.

Norman was a guest on Speech Day, November 1918, at the Boys' High School. Saltaire. (now Salt Grammar School). The Headmaster, M.J. Fuller, spoke of the dark years of the war when many of the older boys and their teachers had lost their lives. He paid tribute to their bravery and self-sacrifice, which had enabled this day of

Peace to be possible. He said, "A great man had told them that they could not have an A1 nation with C3 men and he would remind them that, from an educational point of view, they could not run a scientific nation with thirteen year old education. The Government had passed, without opposition, an Education Bill which was the greatest advance for several decades. The education of a boy was not, and could not, be completed when he was thirteen years old; under the terms of the new Bill a boy would remain at school until he was sixteen and in some cases eighteen. He had heard it said that a boy who went to school till he was sixteen was handicapped as against a boy who had left school and gone to work three years sooner. But the truth was that the boy who had remained at school was able to take opportunities that were not within the reach of the others who had not had the benefit of a longer education, and in one bound he got there before them".

Mr. Fuller then read out the prize list and Mr. Rae distributed the prizes and the certificates. Mr. Rae apologised for his late arrival saying that he had been delayed in London by the triumphal procession from Charing Cross Station to Buckingham Palace of Sir Douglas Haigh. He congratulated Mr. Fuller and the staff on the excellent record of the school in the past year and congratulated the boys who had won prizes. He said he would particularly speak to those who had not won a prize. However much they cheered the winners, they could scarcely fail to feel some sort of slight despondency in their hearts. He would say to them that one of the most valuable qualities to possess was that of judgement. Other qualities of priceless worth were observation, patience, and dogged perseverance. Yet another virtue - and boys did not carry it about on their coat sleeves - was ambition. They must also have self-confidence. But they must not be vain, arrogant or conceited, for these things were offensive. Responsibility was a thing they must not be afraid of. It became easy to carry and it grew into second nature. If they cultivated a love of truth they would increase continually in power and influence.

What the boys did not know was that, before leaving London, Mr. Rae had received a telegram stating that his soldier son, whom he thought to be in France, had been taken to hospital in Bristol that day. He had foregone the longing to go straight to Bristol rather than disappoint them all at Saltaire. The decision to attend the Speech Day and award the prizes reflected the seriousness of Norman Rae's interest and belief in education. Instilled in him was his parents' encouragement and teaching in the days of the Manse in Hanover Street, Batley.

On the 24th April 1918, six months before the conclusion of the War, the Mayor of Batley, David Stubley J.P. had received the following letter from him.
It reads :-

Rossett Green,
Harrogate.

24 April 1918.

Dear Mr. Mayor,

That nation which fails to give the fullest opportunity for the educational development of its gifted children cannot long remain in the front rank of nations. The class in which you and I belong can least afford to share in their neglect. Nature in the bestowal of her gifts knows no class distinction. The most brilliant boy in one of our great public schools in the North today is of very poor parentage. Scholarships alone gave that lad his chance, and will ultimately give to the nation the benefit of his natural genius.

We have lost many brilliant students in the war. Scholarships for girls are as urgently needed as for boys, in order to enable the most gifted of them to qualify for positions in medicine, chemistry and other branches of natural science. My desire to take part in providing some of these stepping stones, so badly needed by the gifted children of this country. For that purpose I am vesting in trustees £10,000, the income to be given to Leaving Scholarships to students who through lack of means cannot fulfil their educational course.

You know my connection with Bradford and Harrogate. These towns have claims on me I have no right to ignore. I propose, therefore, the following division :-

Income from £3,000 to be divided equally between Batley Boys' Grammar School and the Batley Girls' Grammar School.
Income from £4,000 to the Municipal Secondary School for Girls', Bradford.
Income from £3,000 to the Harrogate Secondary School.

You and I were boys together. I am glad you are Mayor of our native town, and that it is my privilege during your term of office to do something towards furthering higher education, a subject so near to my father's heart, and one which he did so much to foster and encourage during his long ministry in Batley. To see the fruit of one's lifetime is surely a goal to be desired.

Yours very truly,

H.Norman Rae.

Norman had accomplished much since his schooldays at Batley Grammar but he was proud of his ties with Batley and the Grammar School. It was a very old establishment dating back to 1612 when the Rev. William Lee, who also endowed the house and garden for the use of the Headmaster, founded it. There were sixty scholars on its register at that time. The school house was re-built in 1818, the funds for its building being raised by the sale of coal from beneath its land. In 1878 the school was moved to its present site and extensions added in 1883 and 1899. Boys destined to be famous had been pupils there, Sir Titus Salt, Sir Owen Richardson - Nobel Prizewinner for Physics - who did so much to forward the development of valves for radio and television, and Dr. Joseph Priestley, the discoverer of oxygen, were amongst the "old boys".

When Norman Rae endowed the scholarship fund, it was reported in the Yorkshire Observer 27th July 1918 that the remark was made, "It will give many a future "Bulldog" (as a student is called), the chance that most of his predecessors would have given their ears to meet. Those of us wrestling with matric and certificate fees will appreciate the meaning for us and will bring home to the whole body what this splendid gift is going to do for the community".

Batley Girls' Grammar School began as Batley Girls' Higher Grade School. The building sited in Field Hill was opened in 1894. In 1905 it acquired the status of Grammar School and continued as such until 1981. At that date its pupils were transferred to Howden Clough to become part of the town's comprehensive system. The Board of Education already provided facilities for girls to train as teachers, but Norman Rae wished to see wider opportunities for girls to obtain University education.

His aim for opportunities for girls was prominent in the awarding of the Bradford Municipal Secondary School Scholarships. A ripple of laughter went round the hall on the 1918 Speech Day at Hanson's Girls' School when he was asked "Why had he taken so much interest in girls and apparently none in the boys of the city?" He replied that there was little outside help for girls who desired to go to University unless they contemplated entering the teaching profession, which he considered the duty of the Board of Education to provide. Apart from obtaining the right to vote, girls had little opportunity for advancement in their chosen careers. He wanted to see higher spheres of labour opened much wider to girls. He did not believe that girls lacked the brainpower of boys. Smiling, he asked, "Where was the man a really clever woman could not get around?"

In conclusion he urged the successful girls to "Make wider the bridge that they had crossed and make it easier for others to come also". £3,000 was invested in the names of trustees so that an income would be available to provide scholarships for boys and girls attending Harrogate Secondary School. Once again, emphasis was made that the same number of awards should be made to girls as well as boys. Other conditions were that a boy or girl must have been at the school for at least three years and to have remained there to about the age of eighteen. Preference would be given to a candidate who would take up a British University residential course leading to a degree in – Medicine, Science, Maths, Engineering, Agriculture, Commerce, Economics, Modern Languages and Modern Studies, but not to a candidate who proposes to become a teacher unless under exceptional circumstances.

Information would be required as to a candidate's ability, application, character and promise, and the suitability of the course from a national point of view. The financial circumstances of the candidate should be such as without a scholarship, a University course would not be possible.

It is interesting to note the choice of Companies chosen for investment in 1920, ie, -

The East Indian Railway Company ....3% Debenture Stock.
The Midland Railway Company......2.5% Preference Stock.
The North Eastern Railway Co...........4% Preference Stock.
London Brighton and South Coast Railway Co. 5% Preference Stock.
London and South Western Railway Co....3.5% Pref. Stock.
Victoria Falls and Transvaal Power Co. Ltd...2.5% Pref. Stock.
Midland Railway Company...............Perpetual Guaranteed Pref. Stock.

It was proposed that the normal value of a "Norman Rae Scholarship" should be £50 per annum for each of three or four years with the possibility of extension to a fifth year if funds allow and circumstances such as the course proposed render it desirable. The value of the Scholarship may be augmented or extra Scholarships given of such value as the committee shall in their discretion decide.

The hope of which Norman Rae had written earlier in his letter to his friend, David Stubley, had been fulfilled :-

"To see the fruit in one's lifetime is surely the goal to be desired".

CHAPTER THREE

Political Career

At the "khaki" election of 1918, when the Liberals had selected him as their Coalition candidate for the Shipley Division, a public meeting was held at Victoria Hall, Saltaire, on Nov. 26th 1918. His lifelong friend, Mr. Theodore Taylor, told the audience of Mr. Rae's outstanding and fearless championship of the rights of the wool industry. The Liberals and the Unionists together with many Labour supporters were determined to give him an overwhelming majority.

When Norman spoke, it was to declare himself in favour of a Coalition Government. He had "Felt that unity was essential all through the war and that the best elements in all our parties should still combine for a solution of the immense problems with which we are faced".

The opposing candidate was Mr. Tom Snowden, Socialist, who, according to newspaper reports of the election, appears to have been a Pacifist. Norman declared himself to be at a loss to understand the people called Pacifists. "I ask, in all calmness, but with great earnestness, what right has a man to have all the benefits England has got through the blood which has been spilt, and the suffering our boys have gone through, if he himself was not prepared to take his part?"

His only son, Norman D. Rae, was a volunteer. He had seen four years of active service and was in France with his

SHIPLEY DIVISION.

CANDIDATURE OF
MR. H. NORMAN RAE.

VOTE FOR

NORMAN RAE.

To the Electors of the Shipley Division.

LADIES AND GENTLEMEN,

When I was invited some three months ago by the unanimous vote of the Liberal Association for the Division, I took the opportunity to point out that in the reconstruction period after peace was signed it would be in the highest interest of the State to secure the services of the best men in all parties, so that in a sense the brains of the country could be pooled and applied to the intricate and complex problems arising out of and after the war. This is still my opinion, so that in my appeal for your suffrages I shall ask for the support on the grounds hereafter mentioned of every section of the electorate without distinction of party.

Peace is now within measurable distance as the result of the brilliant and conclusive triumph of the allied armies and the more unique but not less pronounced achievement of the British fleet.

Election Leaflet.

regiment, the 13th. York and Lancaster, in the front trenches when the Armistice was signed.

If, eighty years later, Norman's views on Pacifism seems harsh, it would be as well to remember the grievous losses suffered by the men of the West Riding. The Bradford Pals in particular were almost annihilated in the battle of the Somme. It was said that there was not a family in the district who had not lost a relative. There were grieving parents who had lost not one son but many. It was certainly not the time to consider Pacifism. Even though the war and the thought of war was detested, it was not of their choosing and it had to be fought and won.

Speaking at Menston a few days later, Mr. Norman Rae, Liberal Coalition Candidate for the Shipley Division addressed the Electors:- "Peace by negotiation was an absolute impossibility. We should not have got the surrender of the German ships, the German army, or the German submarines by negotiation".

The results of the Election were :-
H. Norman Rae.   Coalition 16,700
Tom Snowden.   Socialist 5,590

                                   Majority 11,000

These were difficult years for Lloyd George, the Liberal Prime Minister, and his Coalition Government. Following the split between the two great Liberal politicians Asquith and Lloyd George in 1916, the Liberal Party was somewhat fragmented. The end of the first World War saw Lloyd George becoming more out of favour and Coalition morale extremely low. The Party as a whole lacked leadership. Some Members drifted to the ever-growing ranks of the Labour Party while others joined Bonar Law and the Conservatives. It was Norman Rae's opinion that the Coalition Government was still necessary to overcome the problems which the country faced at the end of hostilities. He felt that it was that only by having a united alliance could aims be achieved.

Prior to the Election of 1918 the Representation of the People Act had been passed and there had been a redistribution of the seats in Parliament. The vote had been extended to all men over the age of twenty-one and to women over the age of thirty who were householders or wives of householders. At the same time, women were made eligible for Membership of the House of Commons. After the Election, the Coalition of Lloyd George Liberals with the Conservatives was maintained but was opposed by the Asquith Liberals and the Labour Members.

There were many post war problems to be solved, not least the question of Home Rule for Ireland. Disorder and unrest prevailed, continuing after 1921 when Lloyd George tried to meet Irish demands by dividing Ireland into two parts. The Protestant counties of the North East were to become Northern Ireland, the rest of the country was to be known as the Irish Free State. This did not meet the wishes of the strong element which still pressed for complete separation from Great Britain.

During this period there is no record of any major speech made by Norman Rae. One correspondent reported him as "Catching the Speaker's eye on numerous occasions". It was once to ask the question recorded in Hansard for the 12. 3. 1919 when he asked:-

"Whether it was the Prime Minister's intention to make an announcement/suggestion regarding the method of celebrating the conclusion of peace, and if so, whether he would bear in mind the desirability of allowing local authorities ample time to consider the matter and make adequate preparations". The Prime Minister replied, "The Government had considered the matter but any answer is yet premature. Local authorities will be given ample time". Perhaps Norman Rae had in mind the recently passed Education Bill by which the National system of education might be improved and extended, a plan which had his wholehearted approval. In fact, Bradford City Council had already decided on a fund to provide for the establishment of scholarships to enable young men and women to have the opportunity of Higher Education. Norman Rae was a prominent benefactor.

Throughout the whole of his Parliamentary career he continued to press for the improvements which he had promised to fight for in his election speeches. Dealing with the subject of old-age pensions he said:-

"The passing of the Act granting pensions was a wise step, one of the greatest blessings of recent legislation, but the age should be reduced to sixty-five years and the pension raised from five shillings to ten shillings per week."

Remembering that few textile workers reached the age of seventy he thought those changes should be made. He asked for better housing conditions for the people saying:-

"We must have homes in which body and mind can live and grow, and I hope that in the new housing schemes, we shall, as far as possible, have homes with gardens. The necessity for allotments has proved a blessing in disguise. There is a far greater good in them, both to the individual and the country than merely comes from the produce grown. A new interest in life is created. An interest in and love of Nature becomes part of the allotment tiller's life and he carries to his home a sense of satisfaction which no other kind of hobby can give him. I hope the new land which has been under cultivation by allotment holders will not be allowed to go back to the waste conditions of pre-war days or even to grass". (This was a reference to the intensive cultivation of land to grow food crops vitally needed to beat the effects of the German blockade.)

He made his views on the length of the working day quite clear :-

"The hours of labour in our textile factories in Yorkshire are too long, especially for women and young people. To commence at 6am. and work until 5.30 at night with an hour and a half for meals, winter and summer alike, cannot be good for the physique or the morals of the textile workers. As applied to women and children, the system is indefensible. I know of the difficulties of the reduction of hours when it carries the reduction of output, but I believe it would be possible to have greater output per hour if the day were made shorter. We cannot live on our home trade; we are a very large exporter of our products, and in neutral markets we must be able to compete, both in quality and price with our competitors in other countries".

The years immediately after the war were ones of high production in industry as manufacturers endeavoured to satisfy the demand for goods which had been difficult to obtain during the war. Britain was dependant upon exports to balance the imports of raw materials and food. The countries which would normally have purchased goods from Britain were themselves impoverished by the ravages of war. There was no one to buy the manufactured goods and gradually firms were forced to close or go on short time, causing mass unemployment. What had started out to be a brave new world saw many of the planned reforms, begun with such good intentions, held up for lack of finance.

The Education Act was carried out in a rather piece-meal fashion. It had been left too much to the discretion of local authorities so that there were irregularities in its application. However, the school leaving age was raised to fourteen, with the proviso that this could be fifteen if any local councils so wished. The need for better education was one of Norman Rae's ideals and one which he constantly strived to achieve.

Industrial discontent continued to spread and in the years 1919 - 21 strikes among the workers were numerous. The Government had taken over the running of the railways and of the mines during the war years and it was now proposing to hand them back to private ownership, much to the workers dismay. The mineworkers demanded an inquiry into the industry and were prepared to strike to obtain this. The rail and Transport Union supported them and there was a general feeling of deep dissatisfaction and unrest. The Coalition Government was becoming increasingly out of favour, the Conservatives saying that it had served its purpose during the war years and that it was now time to return to the Party system. Lloyd George resigned and the Conservative leader, Andrew Bonar Law, became Prime Minister.

It was at this time, late 1921 - 1922, that Norman Rae proved his sterling worth to the people of his constituency of Shipley. A Bill had been introduced and recommended by the Minister of Health proposing to give the City of Bradford and that of Leeds the right to extend their boundaries to include the small neighbouring townships of Baildon, Bingley and Shipley in the case of Bradford: the Calverley, Pudsey and Guiseley areas for Leeds.

The threat of the Bradford extension was an old one and one that had been defeated in 1898. Bradford City Council claimed that it incurred much expense in providing transport and other facilities for Shipley, and that it would be of benefit to Shipley to come under the administration of Bradford. Shipley was well served by a staunch body of men who were determined to uphold the welfare of the townspeople and to refute Bradford's intentions. The means employed and the reasons for the take-over seemed dubious, but it was clearly intended to benefit the Bradford City Council and the Treasurer's Department. It was well known that the Bradford City Council had overspent their yearly estimate by about £880,000, which was equal to a rate of four shillings and sixpence in the pound. It was alleged that the Shipley rates would be collected, only to benefit Bradford!

The worthy Shipley Councillors thought otherwise. Many prominent people gave freely of their time to gather objections and to present the case that Shipley should remain as its own well-managed Urban District. On the other hand, Bradford Councillors were paid for the extra time attending meetings which the furthering of the Extension Bill required. They had already accepted its success as an established fact. When the Bill came up for its Second Reading, contrary to precedent and against legal advice, Shipley's representatives fought against its acceptance.

As M.P. for Shipley Norman Rae had canvassed and lobbied ceaselessly against the Bill in the House of Commons. Setting aside his involvement in general politics, he swayed the opposition of the parliamentary agents to his side, saying at the time :-

"Even if we go down fighting!"

And fight they did! At 11.40 pm. on the 17th of May 1922 the Leeds and Bradford Extension Bill was rejected by a vote of 199 to 57.

The next morning saw much jubilation by the Shipley representatives still in London. But it was on the 19th. May that back in Shipley there was great rejoicing and many congratulations for all concerned. Bells rang in Baildon and flags flew from all the public buildings in Shipley and Bingley. Norman Rae's response to the excitement was, "I am glad it is all over, it has been a lot of work"

Attending a meeting, he explained that at the Second Reading he did not get a chance to speak although he represented the larger portion of the population affected by the Bill. He gave the reason:-

"I was offered by our Chairman, Mr. Lane Fox, the position of moving the rejection of the measure. My reply was that my only wish was to defeat the Bill. I wished Mr. Ratcliffe to speak but would take any part in the debate he thought best in order to attain that end. 'In that case', he said, 'I should very much prefer you to hold yourself in reserve and reply to Sir William and Major Boyd Carpenter'. As you know, I did not get an opportunity of reply, owing to the rules of the House. The division had to be taken at eleven o'clock and Captain Loseby did not sit down until 1 minute to 11pm". It was then that Norman Rae revealed the stratagem he had evolved for the defeat of the Bill. Addressing the Chairman he said: "It will be, Sir, in the recollection of yourself and fellow Councillors, that we had many meetings, not only at Shipley but at Baildon, Guiseley and Yeadon last year - before I went to Australia, how best to defeat the Bill. Amongst our passengers on my homeward voyage from Australia we had an official of the House of Commons. On board ship we discussed the Bill and the best means of defeating it. Long before the voyage was over I was thoroughly well posted in all the intricacy of Parliamentary procedure and my mind was made up as to the course I should advocate being followed. You, Mr. Chairman, and Mr. Learoyd, the Chairman of your Law and Parliamentary Committee - and let me here say how valuable has been your work and advice in the whole matter - will remember that in our first meeting after my return, I strongly urged the blocking of the Bill as long as it could be blocked and finally to decide against it on the Second Reading. You will remember how the proposal of fighting the Second Reading was looked on with doubt if not opposition by some of our chief advisers and how the matter was left over for further consideration; how that if we eventually decided to fight to the end, and that if we were to go under we would at all events go under fighting. Events have fully justified the course we took, bold and risky though it seemed to our advisers". In reporting the speech, the Shipley Times and Express also noted the loud and well deserved applause which followed. When on the 29th May 1922, the Yorkshire Observer, reporting on the annual meeting of the Shipley Division Liberal Association, quoted Norman Rae as saying that the defence of the Bill could lead to possible changes in procedure. He said that "Opponents of the Bill did all they could to persuade Dr. Addison, who was Minister of Health at the time, to defer the introduction of the Bill until the whole matter had been considered and reported upon by a Royal Commission. Dr. Addison had been most autocratic in the way he had met representatives of the opposing authorities, while his suggestions for keeping down expenditure had been in the favour of the cities seeking to extend their boundaries". Mr. Rae also alleged that Bureaucratic influences had been at work to defeat the opposition. The victory they had won was going to have an important influence far beyond the areas concerned locally. He believed that a Committee would be appointed by Parliament and as a result we should not be surprised to see many radical changes brought about".

A Windhill man was heard to comment that, "Bradford thowt she were bahn to tak Windhill in, but

Going to the investiture at Buckingham Palace.

Cartoon of the new Knight.

Windhill has ta'en Bradford in". Loud applause greeted this little aside.

Norman Rae would have said that there was a bit more to it than that!

And so a very satisfactory end to the troublesome Bradford Extension Bill was achieved and the townspeople of Shipley were able to continue and run their own affairs as they had successfully done for generations. The outlook for the British Government and the Members of Parliament was very unsettled. The end of the Lloyd George Coalition saw a partial reconciliation between the Asquith and the Lloyd George Liberals, but not of sufficient strength to fight against a Conservative majority. Andrew Bonar Law became the Conservative Prime Minister for a short time until the next general election, soon to come at the end of 1922.

In June 1922, the Prime Minister's secretary informed Norman Rae to the effect that in the King's Birthday Honours list a knighthood had been conferred upon him. This Honour delighted the people of his Constituency. He had served them well as their M.P. His knowledge of all aspects of the wool trade, both in this country and in Australia had resulted in his being one of a small commission of five appointed by the Government to inquire into the problems arising over the control of wool. In the hierarchy of a district famous for its woollen trade that was indeed a mark of respect. His fairness as an employer and generosity were legendary. His firm stand as a Free Trader and staunch Liberal were well known and acknowledged.

This makes all the more strange the events and misunderstandings which accompanied his eventual re-election in November 1922.

On a Monday evening, early in November, the Shipley Division Liberal Association decided to adopt him as their Liberal Candidate and pledged themselves to do all they possibly could to secure his return. At the same time Sir Norman pledged himself to fight the Election as a Liberal without any qualification whatsoever. He stood as an out and out Free Trader and promised to advocate the repeal of Part 2 of the Safeguarding of Industries Act (which proposed to place tariffs on imported goods so that British manufacturers could not be undercut or the market swamped by foreign goods). He further declared that unless he was allowed to use his own judgement, if returned to Parliament, he would not stand as Candidate.

The next day, Tuesday, The Shipley Division, Conservative and Unionist Executive Committee held a meeting at the Shipley Unionist Club, inviting Sir Norman to attend. The offer was accepted, and after hearing that Sir Norman was prepared to support Mr. Bonar Law's Government as the only alternative to a Socialist one, so long as the Government passed no reactionary measures, the Conservatives decided provisionally to support Sir Norman and not bring out a candidate to oppose him.

So, having so much support, the next thing Sir Norman had to do was appoint his agent. When asked by Mr. A. Cousin of the Liberal Association about this, Sir Norman said that he was having his own solicitors, though when telephoned, they replied that they would not undertake the agency. He then asked three separate Liberal solicitors in turn but got a refusal from all of them. They said that the remuneration did not make the trouble worth while. He then consulted his own solicitors again and they suggested the name of Mr. Macguiness. When telephoned he replied, "I am somewhat indifferent". Seeing his predicament, the Conservatives magnanimously placed the services of their agent, Mr. S.H. Servant, at his disposal to assist in securing his return as the Liberal candidate.

On the Wednesday evening, on hearing this, many members of the Liberal Association proclaimed indignation. In Bingley it was said that the feeling of the majority was that Sir Norman had decided to look to the Official Unionist Party machinery as his working body and not that of the Liberal Party. Furthermore, the information had been given that an Independent Liberal of good standing and convinced Liberalism, was prepared to come forward for the position of Liberal candidate. In the space of three days there was a split in the Shipley Division. A vote was taken, and by a marked majority the resolution was accepted to adopt Mr. Arthur Davy as the Independent Liberal candidate. Sir Norman said he would stand as a National Liberal, supporting Free Trade as he had always done.

When the nominations were handed in at the Shipley Council Office on the Saturday, the candidates were as follows :-

Arthur Davy. (Ind. Lib.) of Blakeney Grange. Wyke. Wool merchant. Proposers and seconders included James Cousin, Harold Watson, George Albert Newboult, John W.

Sir H. N. Rae with grand-daughter Marion Jean Woodhead and grandson Norman Woodhead at Rossett Green, Harrogate.

The week-end retreat at Buckden, known affectionately to the family as 'The Hut'.

Denby, E.E. Airey, Joseph W. Walker, Samuel Brown, Kate Slicer, and Fanny Harrison.

Sir H.N. Rae. (Nat. Lib.) of Rossett Green, Harrogate. Wool merchant. Proposers and seconders included Charles W. Wade, John W. Sowden, John Henderson, Herbert Sutcliffe, John H. Robinson, J.A. Burton, Lady Ella Peel, Jonas Hanson, Frank Parkinson, Christina Denison, Reginald Bailey, Thomas W. Walker, Abraham Hopwood, Charles E. Clarke, J.H. Widdop, and Harold Holmes.

William Mackinder (Lab.) 12, Kirkstone St. Bradford. Trade Union Secretary. Proposers and seconders included Thomas H. Grange, Benjamin Scott, Henry Wilson, Mathew Coleman, Mary Kendal, Mary J. Jordan, Annie Grange, Emma Henderson, Annie Ives, Mary Little. Ivy E. Midgley and Hannah Haigh.

The result of the poll was :-

Sir H. Norman Rae. (Nat. Lib.) 12,201

W. Mackinder.   (Soc. Lab.)..... 11,160

Arthur Davy.   (Ind. Lib.)..... 6,674

Sir H. Norman Rae, having a clear majority, was returned as National Liberal M.P. for the Shipley Division at the Nov. 1922 election.

The Conservatives had obtained a clear Party majority for the first time since 1900. Although there had been a majority of their members after the previous general election, some had been elected as members of a Coalition,

Liberals voting for Conservatives in some divisions and Conservatives supporting Liberals in others. Andrew Bonar Law remained as Prime Minister until ill-health forced his resignation in the early summer of 1923. His had been a short period of office with little activity taking place, and with his resignation came the problem of his replacement. Lord Curzon, the Foreign Secretary, was the most experienced Conservative leader with long and distinguished service to the Party and his country, but he was in the House of Lords. It was felt that the conditions and changes of the times could make Government from the House of Lords very difficult.

With the Labour Party now as the official opposition, there were many questions being raised concerning the welfare of the working classes. King George V, after consulting leading statesmen, passed over Lord Curzon in favour of Stanley Baldwin. His first Administration was very short lived however. Unemployment was at a high level and Baldwin decided that the only way to protect jobs and industry was to introduce protective tariffs. Even with a majority in the Commons, the Government had no mandate from the electorate for such a departure from Free Trade traditions. Baldwin appealed to the country but in the general election of December 1923 all proposals of protection were rejected.

At this last election of 1923, Sir Norman intimated that, now Liberal unity had been achieved, he wished to retire from politics. When he received numerous telegrams urging him to reconsider his decision, and pressure came from the Liberal headquarters hoping that he would change his mind, he gave all requests careful consideration. Then

THE
SHOPPING CARNIVAL

Will be opened in the

MARKET PLACE, SHIPLEY,

Thursday, June 7th at 3 o'clock,

BY THE

Vice-Chairman of the

Urban District Council,

COUNCILLOR A. C. MARSDEN.

Chair will be taken by

SIR NORMAN RAE, M.P.

Who will be supported by representatives of the Chamber of Trades, Public Bodies, etc.

The Opening will be signified by the release of Balloons

The Yorkshire Military Band

will play in the Market Place from 2-30 to 5 p.m.

Conductor: Mr. Albert Carpenter.

Booklet, Shipley Shopping Carnival, 1923.

on the morning of the 15th November 1923, he informed his two whips, Sir Arthur Marshall and Sir William Edge, that his previous views remained unchanged. Having worked so hard for the good of his Constituency and having achieved so much, this was his last Parliament. There were many who were saddened by his decision. He was now sixty - three years old.

SHIPLEY SHOPPING CARNIVAL
7th - 16th JUNE 1923.

Sad though the news was of Sir Norman's retirement from Parliamentary duties, the year of 1923 was a brighter one for the people of Shipley. The threat of the City Extension Bill had been removed, and the much-dreaded absorption of the town by Bradford had been defeated. Shipley had grown from the small number of 1,926 inhabitants in 1831, to 29,000 in 1922. Unemployment was still a factor, and there was a plea by the Town Council to Shipley tradespeople to encourage trade to the town from the surrounding districts, by offering a wide selection of good quality merchandise at reasonable prices.

The challenge was taken up by the Shipley Chamber of Trade. The proposal was to hold a Shopping Carnival, a bright and entertaining affair which would dispel the doldrums and present Shipley in a new and prosperous light. Mr. Alfred Cousin of Manor Lane, Shipley, took on the task of compiling and editing a handbook on the history of Shipley. In it he states that "The history of the town from 1066A.D. up to one hundred years ago, (1823), is so meagre that there is little or no interest in it for the present generation." With photographs by Mr. H. Sayner of Saltaire Road, the book was still judged to make very interesting reading.

Sir Norman Rae was asked to preside at the opening ceremony and replied from the House of Commons;

"Dear Mr. Feather,

I am much obliged to your committee for asking me to be Chairman on June 7th. If it will be agreeable to you to accept me as Chairman subject to being able to get away from here, I would gladly accept. You quite understand that we cannot always manage to fulfil mid-week engagements.

I hope your Carnival will be a success".

(signed.) H.N.R.

The well-planned event was a great success. A Mr. C.E.Wyatt of London, who was much experienced in the staging of such ventures, was appointed as adviser. He promptly doubled the number of advertising balloons to be released from five to ten gross, while flags and bunting were to make a bright display everywhere. One of the innovations of the Carnival week was the appointment of a Mystery Man - a "Mr. Carnival" - who carried a number of vouchers which he awarded to any successful person who recognised and challenged him. Schoolchildren were encouraged to enter an essay writing competition, with prizes offered for the best essay on "A walk through Shipley, Saltaire and Windhill during the Shopping Carnival." Many other competitions were arranged but the most sought after man in Shipley that week was certainly "Mr. Carnival" !

It was recorded that Sir Norman arrived in time for the opening in Shipley Market Place on Thursday, June 7th. With him on the platform were representatives of the Chamber of Trades and other Public Bodies. The balloons floated up to the clouds, and the Yorkshire Military Band, conducted by Mr. Albert Carpenter, played from 2.30pm. - 5.00pm.

Shipley once again, was asserting itself as a very independent, go-ahead small town.

CHAPTER FOUR

The Gift of Northcliffe

When, in 1919, some land and properties in Shipley, estates of the late 5th. Earl of Rosse, were put up for auction, the Northcliffe fields and woods were offered as lots 98 and 99. Under the title "Freehold building estate" the agent gave details which included "A useful agricultural occupation - known as North Cliff Farm with well equipped farm buildings, North Cliff Cottage with garden and newly slated workshop occupied by the Estate Woodman, water being supplied from a spring. Each lot to include parts of North Cliff Wood". The whole area being described as, "Together forming a freehold building estate for the development of garden suburbs, an area of picturesquely undulating surface, bounded on the South side by a wide belt of natural woodland of great beauty".

However, at the end of the auction, lots 98 and 99 remained unsold. Shipley Council had previously expressed an interest in purchase, and the late Earl had left instructions that if the Council decided to buy the North Cliff Estate, especially low terms were to be granted to them. The price was £12,500 for 114 acres of land, much of it suitable for building purposes. It was too tempting an offer to refuse but the Council needed a loan to make the purchase. Subject to the approval of the Ministry of Health, it was proposed to provide a park and playing fields, with a considerable area given over to allotments, (the present allotments being earmarked for building land). Houses were to be built on another part of the estate.

Spring Morning in North Cliff Woods

OPENING OF THE NORTH CLIFF WOODS
AND THE
NORMAN RAE PLAYING FIELDS,

Mr. H. Norman Rae, M.P., & Mrs. Rae
request the pleasure of your Company
at 2-30 p.m., on Saturday, June 12th, 1920,
at the North Cliff Woods, Shipley,
for the Opening Ceremony, which will be performed
by their grand-daughter, Miss Marion Jean Woodhead.

Invitation to the opening ceremony, 12th June 1920.

The golden key which was presented to her. (This is now on permanent display in the Council Chamber, Town Hall, Shipley)

One Friday, after hearing of the sale, Norman Rae decided to walk over the site with the Chairman of the District Council, Mr. H. Hirst, and the Clerk, Mr. L. Lindow. He was "Greatly impressed by its advantages both for allotments and recreative purposes". Before leaving Shipley that evening, he intimated that he might offer to bear the cost of the purchase. He later confirmed this partial promise, and as he had an engagement in Shipley on the next evening, Saturday, a special meeting of the Council was held on the Saturday afternoon. The only condition that he made was that the whole of the estate should be devoted to the benefit of the public. This action fulfilled Norman Rae's own dream of bringing the countryside nearer to the people for their own pleasure and relaxation. The Chairman then moved a resolution accepting the gift with pleasure and gratitude, undertaking that the estate should be preserved entirely for the benefit of the public.

Later, when opening an exhibition of the Shipley Gardeners and Allotment Holders Association, Norman Rae spoke of his inspection of the Rosse Estate. He said, "I was greatly impressed by the beauties of that estate. You have here woodland in its most natural and wildest state. It cannot be surpassed for beauty in Yorkshire. There is a portion too which is ideal for allotment holders and I am pleased to know that those who are now being dispossessed of their allotments will be able to get permanent holdings on this estate".

After the immediate euphoria had subsided it was time to plan the conversion of the newly acquired estate. Most of the land was under cultivation by the farmer and growing crops, until harvested, delayed much alteration.

There was a nine hole golf course at the Moorhead end of the fields, played over by Shipley Golf Club. It had been in use since 1897, (traces of the old tees and greens can still be seen on the playing fields.)

It is always intriguing, when planning a new development, to wonder what had gone before, in that old building or on that old land, and North Cliff was old land. The whole area had been in private ownership since the earliest record of local history. In 1042 A.D. an Anglo Saxon, Ravenschil, was Lord of the Manor of Shipley. A few years later came the Norman Conquest and the small township of Shipley, together with the hamlet which is now Moorhead, part of Heaton Royds, Shipley Fields and Saltaire became the property of Ilbert de Lacy. According to the history books the land seems to have been an ill-gotten gain. The time was known as the "Harrying of the North" a barbaric massacre of the inhabitants by Ilbert's men, a reprisal ordered by William the Conquerer to quell the rebellious Anglo Saxons. Ilbert's reward was a hundred and fifty manors situated in a stretch of land between the Aire and the Calder. Bradford had been left waste, one can only imagine the terrible destruction and loss of life which this caused. It was to take many generations before the population recovered to anything like its previous number.

If we take a leap in time to around 1840, the town of Bradford was growing to accommodate the fast increasing textile trade. Coal to fire the steam power in the mills was much in demand. Around the district small mines began to be developed, the richest of the Shipley collieries was the outcrop at Shipley High Moor, with workings in Old

Spring Woods and North Cliff. An Ordinance Survey map of 1852 shows the area dotted with the sites of small coal mines, many of them owned by the Jackson family who were then the Lords of the Manor. Day holes or bell pits can still be seen as green depressions in both North Cliff and Spring woods. The mines must have been either worked out or become unprofitable because the land was eventually given over to agriculture. Tythe maps of the period show fascinating field names, - Six Days Work for a sizeable plot, with Two Days Work applying to a small strip. "High" and "Low" Blue Close, Scarpe Close - quite large - must have been a hilly location.

On the 21st May 1920, the minutes of the Cemetery and Parks Committee record the meeting held at the Branch Farm for the purpose of deciding as to the approach roads and fences for the allotments on the Rosse Estate. After traversing the distance, it was agreed that the existing stone fences (walls?) on the West side of the cricket field, at Cliff Wood Mount be removed and used for the pitching of the road to the allotments, and that a post and rail fence be erected on the line of the new road to protect the farmer's crops on land which was not yet available for playing fields.

The Committee afterwards visited North Cliff Woods, (note the spelling, the appended "e" seems to occur at a much later date) and gave instructions for the foot paths for the use of the public to be indicated by the laying of bark. All the branch footpaths were to be connected to the main path through the wood and one leading from Redburn to High Bank be constructed. Forty loads of bark were used on the footpaths, seventy loads of soil and eight hundred yards of sods, taken from various parts of the estate, had been laid to extend the levelled portion of the meadow near to the Keeper's cottage. Seats for the use of the public were to be suitably placed on the footpaths and warning notices to be erected in various parts of the wood indicating that the public should not leave the footpaths. This last edict was most strictly enforced by the zealous Keeper, as were the picking of wild flowers or the removal of plants. At Norman Rae's suggestion the bare mounds of earth (shale?) in the woods were to be covered in soil and sown with grass seed, and the turfing of the field at the South entrance to be completed. The Committee considered a scheme for the provision of toilets to be built on the West side of the wood and recommended that the water main, gas main and sewer be extended from Redburn Avenue to the Keeper's cottage. The Surveyor was instructed to prepare a plan. As the official opening date had already been agreed as the 12th June 1920, when Norman Rae would officially hand over the deeds of the Rosse Estate to the Council, barely three weeks away, there must have been much concentrated work put in by the Council workmen. It was decided that the opening ceremony take place at the new wooden gates by the Keeper's cottage at the entrance to the woods. (The large imposing wrought iron main gates at the entrance to the playing fields were erected at a later date).

Elaborate plans were made for the opening ceremony. About 4,000 schoolchildren from the Elementary Schools had been invited and were to meet at the Otley Road Council School. Then, led by the Shipley Band, they walked in procession to North Cliff Wood where they assembled on the meadow. Crowds of local people

School children arriving for opening of Northcliffe, June 12th 1920.

Entrance to Northcliffe Woods.

thronged the pathway to the wood and waited for the Ceremony to begin. Norman Rae was accompanied by Mrs. Rae, family members, Council Officials, the Lord and Lady Mayoress of Bradford and many other dignitaries, amongst them Mr. Theodore C. Taylor, his old friend from the Congregational Church at Batley. It was a beautiful summer day as his young grand-daughter, Miss Marion Jean Woodhead declared the woods "Open". In the photograph taken at the time, she looks very small but completely self-possessed as she displays the golden key presented to her as a memento by Mrs. Fearnley Rhodes on behalf of Shipley Council. Her three year old brother, Norman, looks very serious, the enormous crowd must have made the occasion rather daunting. Mrs. Rae was presented with a lovely bouquet of roses by one of the youngest scholars.

Norman Rae spoke feelingly of the thoughts and wishes which were in his mind and heart as he handed over the deeds of the Estate to the Chairman, Mr. F. Fearnley Rhodes. He remarked that the amassing of wealth merely for the love of wealth was a sorry business at the best. By the use we made of our opportunities, whether by deed or by gift, we must be judged. It had been one of his privileges to travel a great deal, and as he had viewed some of the wonder scenes of the world he had wished that he could bring them nearer to the inhabitants of our great cities. He was particularly anxious that the beauty of this spot be maintained in the same delightful state as when it was in private ownership. A short time before, an "elected" group of schoolchildren had accompanied him through a tour of the woodland and had pledged that neither they nor their school-fellows would interfere with

Presentation of the gold key to Miss Marion Jean Woodhead at the opening of Northcliffe Woods, June 12th 1920.

the bird life or other natural beauties of the woodland. The large gathering that day was the sequel to a walk he had taken nearly a year ago. The thought had come to him then, that - "These are the woods and fields you should take your part in opening and preserving for the public good".

He was told that from the surrounding woods the ferns and flowers had disappeared and that the singing birds had sought fresh homes. It was his earnest desire that North Cliff Woods be spared such a fate. In urging the children to lead unselfish lives, he said that in after years their greatest reward would not be the praise of others, but an inward consciousness that they had done what they could for human betterment.

Loud applause greeted him at the end of his speech, increasing in volume as he requested that the schoolchildren be given a half-day holiday that they might enjoy their new possession. It was a happy crowd of children who proceeded to the marquees where tea had been provided for them. One of those children, when asked, eighty years later, if he could describe Norman Rae, paused for a moment then said quietly, "He was a gentle man".

And so began a busy period of completing the change from farming land to playing fields. It was thought desirable that the fields should bear the title – "The Norman Rae Playing Fields", the woods would retain the name North Cliff Woods. The whole of the area was fast becoming a well used amenity, rivalling the well known Shipley Glen in popularity. According to the season, football or other games were played in the fields, while

Opening speech, Northcliffe, June 12th 1920.

throughout the year the woodland walk was thronged with people, all obediently keeping to the paths. A shallow boating or paddling pool was constructed a little way beyond the meadow. A well built shelter, quartered with broad seats and sheltering glass panels, made it possible for mothers to keep an eye on their offspring as they played in the pool. Another shelter of the same design was erected on a high point in the playing fields, providing a welcome haven when rain threatened.

In May 1923 a further attraction was added to the woodland. Shipley Council had long been pressed to provide a bandstand to enable concerts to be held on Sunday evenings. The new bandstand had been specially designed by their surveyor, Mr. Herbert Dawson, to meet the requirements of the situation. Built by Messrs. Petty and Holt of Shipley it was rectangular in shape, 28ft. 6ins. long by 15ft. 3ins. in depth. It incorporated a semi-circular sounding board to ensure perfect acoustic properties. With electricity installed it was suitable for concerts or open air functions. The cost was estimated at £450. The Yorkshire Military Band was engaged to play for the opening concert on Sunday 25th May, their conductor was Mr. Albert Carpenter. Rain began to fall just before the time arranged for the opening ceremony. Mr. George Birbeck, Chairman of the Shipley Urban District Council, in introducing Sir Norman Rae, said that they were all delighted that their Member was able to be with them that afternoon. Whenever they made any additions to North Cliff Woods it was only fitting that Sir Norman should be present, (there was mutual assent at this remark). The Council had tried to provide a bandstand in keeping with the beautiful woods and that it was their intention to

The Paddling Pool, North Cliff Woods

provide high-class musical performances and had engaged the following bands to give concerts during the season, Shipley Brass Band, The Seaforth Highlanders, Blue Imperial, Halifax Police, United Services Band (Bradford), Bradford Police, Bradford Post Office, and Armley and Wortley Brass Band.

Perhaps the popularity of these concerts prompted a letter written to the Town Clerk. It was from the Representatives of the Anglican and Free Churches at Shipley. – "This Meeting being fully convinced that in the interests of the mental, physical and spiritual well-being of the people of Shipley, it is absolutely vital to preserve the character of Sunday as a day of Worship and Renewal. We respectfully urge the Urban District Council to take such steps as may be necessary to safeguard the sacred traditions of our English Sunday, and in particular not to allow music in the parks at such times as will infringe on the usual hours of Divine Service and of any instruction in Sunday Schools. Also not to encourage or allow games in public places which would militate against the quietude which the vast majority of the inhabitants of Shipley wish to enjoy on the day of rest." The Committee were generally in agreement with the terms of the letter and the Clerk was asked to point out that arrangements had been made for the Band Performances not to commence before 7-30pm on Sunday evenings.

In June 1926 an event, significant in Church circles, was held in the woods. It was the first of five planned united Church services, aimed at creating better unity and understanding between various denominations. Ministers and representatives of the District's many churches spoke to a large congregation of the need for Christian unity. The Rev. N.H. Harding Jolly, vicar of Shipley, said they had come into the open air and he considered this a step in the right direction. They wanted to break the old spirit of prejudice and unkindness, which had come down to them from the past and feel that in this new age they could stand by one another as brethren. The Salvation Army Band accompanied the congregation. The collection was in aid of local hospitals.

For some time it had become noticeable that there had been a deviation in the old way of spelling the name of the woods. From the original "North Cliff" it occasionally became "Northcliff", now and again the appended "e" became apparent. Gradually this became acceptable and most people wrote and spoke of the woods as "Northcliffe". But however the spelling of the name, it continued to be the pride and joy of the people of Shipley. The local schools used the football and hockey pitches for their inter-house matches, and local societies were granted the use of the woods for their various activities. There was a good attendance when the Rev. J.S. Crole addressed a Meeting for the League of Nations, and the United Male Voice Choir Concerts sounded well in the acoustically balanced new bandstand. Eventually, tennis courts were created at the lower, Bradford Road end of the fields. They were hard courts, nestling into the fall of the hillside, with sheltered seats to enable spectators to view the games in comfort. A pavilion and toilets adjoining, and a little later a bowling green, made this a popular place, either for a game or to be a spectator. Northcliffe seemed to be able to cater for all needs, there was the "space" so accurately pin-pointed by Sir Norman, and with such heartfelt gratitude by all who used it.

So it was with much concern that the Park Ranger reported that some members of the public were causing wilful damage in the woods, (the offenders names were before the Committee) and that with the present number of staff it was difficult to patrol the whole area. Help was soon forthcoming however, the clerk reported that a number of residents in the neighbourhood of Northcliffe were willing to act as Wardens in the woods to "assist in the preservation of the beauties of the woods for the benefit of the public". He read the names of the 22 gentlemen who had so kindly volunteered their services as wardens of the woods. The Committee also intimated that future cases of transgression would be brought before the Magistrates. The volunteer Wardens must have done their work well because an item in later Council Minutes thanks them for their services which were now deemed unnecessary. The post of Warden was held for many years by one of the farmers whose land had been acquired for the playing fields. His house, North Cliff Farm, was later to become the meeting room of the Bowling Club.

"Northcliffe" became a well-loved place, guarded with a sense of propriety and gratitude by the townsfolk of Shipley.

CHAPTER FIVE

The Norman Rae Nursing Home

The building which is now Shipley Hospital is built on an area of land once called Whitcliffe and which was owned by a Mr. Bateman.

A triangular piece of land, it was bounded on the North by Church Lane (now Kirkgate), Rossendale Place to the South West, and what is now Wellington Crescent to the East. Originally it was divided into three parcels, Near Whitcliffe where the hospital stands, Whitcliffe in the centre and far Whitcliffe nearest to Wellington Crescent.

Near Whitcliffe eventually came into the ownership of the Denby family, Worsted Spinners, of Tong Park. It was John Denby (Sir Ellis' brother), who commissioned the building of a handsome residence, Whycliffe House, for his own use, but it was Sir Ellis and William Denby who lived there prior to their removal to Grassington. The house then became the Whycliffe Residential Hotel, owned by Miss Marion Best.

When the hotel came up for sale in 1922, Sir Norman Rae M.P. realised its potential as a "Much needed Maternity Home for the women of Shipley and Bradford". It was to be a reasonably priced facility coming between the public hospital and the private nursing home. The charge would be four guineas a week and it was Sir Norman's intention that the fees should cover the working expenses.

With this purpose in mind, he generously purchased and equipped it as an up to date maternity hospital. When the conversion was completed the new hospital was declared free from all debt or capital charges. Miss Scott, Deputy Matron of York Maternity Home, was appointed Matron.

The official opening day was arranged for the 4th September 1923. Crowds gathered in Church Lane to welcome H.R.H. Princess Mary (Viscountess Lascelles) who was going to perform the opening ceremony. The Princess was a very popular Royal personage and the people of Shipley and district were eager to give her an enthusiastic welcome. The Shipley Times and Express records the event in its columns:-

"At one o'clock tramcars began to bring large numbers of folk into the centre of Shipley, and between two and three o'clock the trams from Idle and Thackley were absolutely packed", in fact, the tramcars could not hold all those who wanted to see the Princess, and charabancs were run to accommodate the crowds. Shortly before the time of Princess Mary's arrival the lower part of Otley Road (from Baildon Bridge) the Fox and Hounds corner to Commercial Street presented a busy sight, people being stationed two and three deep on each side of the road, several of the mills having released their workpeople for half-an-hour. Children were also very much in evidence, the Shipley schools having been closed for the afternoon in honour of the occasion".

As the Royal entourage arrived at the Hospital, a contingent of the Bradford and District Girl Guides formed

Arrival of H.R.H. Princess Mary at the Nursing Home.

Controlling the crowds.

Sir H. N. Rae excorting H.R.H. Princess Mary opening of Nursing Home.

Sir H. N. Rae giving his opening speech.

"Where is the key?"

a guard of honour. Photographs of the event show a very proud, but perhaps a little nervous, Sir Norman welcoming the Princess. The photograph shows Sir Norman, right hand tentatively in jacket pocket: under the photograph he has written "Where is the Key?"

In his speech at the beginning of the ceremony Sir Norman said that one of the chief features of the Royal House had been and was at the present time, the anxiety its Members displayed to alleviate suffering in every form, and to honour those who devoted their lives to the Christian Ministry . "May I say," he continued, "that your Royal Highness's well known devotion to the cause of the sick and helpless is especially emphasised by your personal experience of the self-sacrificing duties of a nurse. In coming to open this Home you have shown once more the human sympathy and interest we have learnt to associate with you, and your kindness will inevitably strengthen the bond that binds you to all".

"We Yorkshire folk have many qualities which may appear strange to your Royal Highness. We are blunt of speech, rough and ready in our manners, and apt to show our worst side to those who come amongst us as strangers. But we have warm hearts and our gruff speech is often the cloak that hides our tender emotions. Yet no section of the community is quicker to recognise true kindness, none is quicker to distinguish sincere sympathy, and none more ready to welcome and acknowledge it. Your Royal Highness had a warm place in the affections of Yorkshire folk before you gave us the opportunity to know you more intimately by making your home in our midst. We esteemed you for your work's sake when we simply shared

H.R.H. The Princess Royal signing the Visitors Book at the opening of the Norman Rae Nursing Home, Shipley, September 4th 1923.

THIS NURSING HOME
was Opened on September 4th, 1923, by
H.R.H. PRINCESS MARY
(VISCOUNTESS LASCELLES)

Mary.

Entries in the Norman Rae Nursing Home Visitors Book.

you as our Princess with the rest of England. Now that your home is amongst us and you are the mother of a Yorkshire boy, we have noted how you have identified yourself with the interest of our county. We ask you, Princess of our Royal House and daughter of our loved and honoured Queen," concluded Sir Norman, "to perform the opening ceremony".

In doing so the Princess said, with simple sincerity, "I have much pleasure in declaring the Home open. I wish it the success which it thoroughly deserves".

Sir Norman then presented the Princess with a gold key with which to open the main door. The key bore on one side the inscription "The Norman Rae Nursing Home, opened by Princess Mary (Viscountess Lascelles) September 4th 1923". The reverse of the key was enamelled with the Royal Arms and Princess Mary's own bars superimposed.

After unlocking the door she was conducted through the wards by the Matron, Miss Scott and Dr. M.S. Sharp (Chairman of the Ladies Committee). In one ward was the Home's first patient, a proud mother with her two week old son. The Princess made enquiries concerning their progress for which she expressed her good wishes. She was greatly impressed with the conversion from the hotel to hospital. There were eight bedrooms with a total of twenty-four beds. A report in the Shipley Times reads :- "To the left of the hall is the largest ward accommodating five beds, a lofty restful room whose walls are colour-washed in a warm stone shade. The windows, in common with the rest of the house are curtained in dark green. The second ward on the opposite side of the hall will accommodate three beds, but for this occasion was elegantly furnished as a retiring room for the Princess. Next to it is a capacious linen room and ward three which accommodates four maternity cases. A beautiful room this, with pretty pale green walls and elaborately ornamental ceiling. In all the rooms remain as they were during the occupation of the house as a private residence. Ward four, with stone coloured walls, effectively cool-looking with the green curtains, is prepared for more maternity cases. Next door is an airy nursery, alternately a room where doctors may interview patients. At the other side of the corridor are the domestic offices, the Matron's office and the Nurses' combined dining and sitting room, its walls washed in a shade of terracotta that suggest cosy comfort. Mounting the staircase and taking the rooms to the right, there is a smaller ward with green decorations, the sterilising room and the spotlessly white operating theatre with its soundproof doors. There is in addition, the Sister's bedroom and the Matron's bright little bed-sitting room. At the end of this corridor is the isolation room and on the opposite side of it, the staff's bathroom. To the right a lift connects with the kitchen and a staircase leads to the Cook's, Maids' and Night Nurses' rooms, while the corridor ends at the patients' bathrooms".

When the tour was over and the Ladies' Committee had been presented to the Princess, she was photographed on the front steps of the Home. It was here that Sir Norman's little grand-daughter, Miss Marion Jean Woodhead, presented the Princess with a bouquet of lemon coloured carnations. Sir Norman's grand-daughter (the late Mrs. Hofer who lived in Switzerland) wrote on the 25th

Miss Marion Jean Woodhead presented a bouquet to H.R.H. Princess Mary.
Left to Right - Back Row
Sir Norman Rae, Lady-in-Waiting - Dorothy Yorke (Pateley Bridge), Matron -
Miss Scott, Dr Margaret Sharpe, Surgeon - Mr Jason Wood.
Left to Right - Front Row
Miss Jean Woodhead, H.R.H. Princess Mary, Mr. F. H. Fawkes, M.P., Lady Rae.

Oct.1995 :- "I remember standing on the platform with the other guests, having our photo' taken. I was holding a bouquet I was to present to Princess Mary and she told me to hold the bouquet lower, otherwise my face would be hidden. I also remember there was one mother with her new-born baby, the first patient. I was disappointed not to be taken to see the baby".

It was a day for which everyone who attended had their own special memories, a day of sunshine, cheering crowds and flags and bunting flying everywhere. Generations of Shipley and district's children were to be born there. The Norman Rae Nursing Home, its name synonymous with care and kindness, was held in great affection by thousands of the area's residents.

A footnote to this account :- On the 4th September 1996, the Hospital was re-opened after a major re-fitting and re-building programme. Its new function is to provide short stay re-habilitation for people who have had treatment in the larger hospitals but still need greater support than is available in their own homes. The conversion has been expertly and beautifully accomplished.

Mr. Norman Woodhead, the grandson of Sir Norman Rae, performed the opening ceremony.

The ceremony and re-opening of Shipley Hospital was, to Shipley people, a continuation of what had been a legend.

CHAPTER SIX

The Northcliffe Golf Club

In 1921 the Shipley Golf Club whose members played over the nine hole golf course at the Moorhead end of North Cliff, obtained land for a new eighteen hole course at Beckfoot, Bingley, and in doing so, vacated the land on North Cliff which was rented from Shipley Council.

This seemed to be a good opportunity to form a Northcliff Golf Club, an idea which had the enthusiastic backing of Norman Rae. Support was soon forthcoming from over two-hundred people anxious to become members. The first game was played on the 1st August 1921. By October the newly formed club had purchased part of the Shipley Golf Club's former Club House and re-erected it on their own site. Very soon, Norman Rae was again a benefactor and bought a further acreage of land to enable the newly formed Club to play over eighteen holes; eight on the North Cliff field and the new ten across the ravine.

There was, however, more than a little dissatisfaction over two of the Council's stipulations. No golf could be played on the Sabbath on the first eight holes because they were on Council land and no alcoholic beverage could be sold in the Club House because it too was so affected. The latter decree was prohibited because it was in the Deed of Gift between Norman Rae and the Council, (12th June 1920); it is interesting to note that in the 1980's an application to hold a Pop-Music Festival in Northcliffe fields failed because of this stipulation against the sale of alcohol. On Sundays, Members were restricted to playing on the unaffected ten holes which had been purchased by Norman Rae.

In October 1921 the Club decided to re-furbish and re-erect the Club House; it was officially opened in June 1922 by Sir Norman (he was knighted in June 1922) as President of the Northcliff Golf Club. He was asked to accept a memento of the occasion which was a silver golf ball mounted on a tripod of golf clubs and inscribed as follows – "Presented to Sir Norman Rae, M.P. President, on the occasion of the opening of the Northcliff Golf Club, June 24th 1922." Thanking the Chairman, Sir Norman replied, "I have one gift that I keep at home," he said "and much as I shall value this one, I almost think that I value the one at home more than any other gift. It was given to me by 3,000 children from the Elementary schools of Shipley. Next to that I shall value this gift of yours, mainly because of its associations with what I believe will prove to be, in time to come, of great value to the inhabitants of this district. If open spaces are not saved when they are open spaces - and I confess that present time seems necessary to get possession of them - they are lost forever. I am glad that these open spaces are reserved for sports and playing ground, and, shall I say, walking ground for so many of the people of Shipley. Some months ago," Sir Norman continued, "I brought a Member of the present Government to look at your golf links and these woods. I told him what a beautiful site it was, and what a beautiful view he would have from the top. Unfortunately, it was one of those days of fog right over the valley and we could see no further than those trees. Only this week when we were in the House of Commons until four o'clock on Wednesday morning, I think it was about half-past three, my friend said, "How's Norman's view looking now?"

"There are many games," continued Sir Norman, "wherever the English speaking people lived that were played, but he knew of no game that had the same characteristics as golf. It seemed to him to have much wider attractions than any other game, and when on such links as these they had time to admire the view, especially when they got bunkered! Cricket was universally played wherever the English language was spoken, but it was essentially a game for the young. He remembered seeing a cricket match played during the Boer War which was one of the strangest sights he ever saw. There were eleven Boers on either side and "Tommies" on the opposite side of the pitch with their rifles and bayonets fixed, but that did not seem to disturb those cricketers. Then we had tennis - essentially a game for the young - though in Earl Balfour they had one who still enjoyed a game in spite of being seventy years of age. Baseball, the great national game of America, was essentially a game for professionals, but it has always been my desire to help forward games that were played by members rather than professionals". Cheers greeted this last remark. "Then there was bowling," added Sir Norman, "which they tell me is my game - the old man's game - and lastly there is golf - the ancient and royal game of golf - which I have already said, has attractions wider than any one of those games I have mentioned. It is a manly, healthful recreation, and as an exercise equally adaptable for the old, middle aged and young. It knows no distinction of sex; there is in it full play for the overflowing exuberance of youth as well as the matured and tempered strength of manhood. I think it has more devotees of the gentler sex amongst its members than any other game in the world." He continued, "I have always thought that in spite of the fact that you don't belong to the gentler sex, that there is something in the swing of a lady's stroke which can never be copied by man". There was laughter at this remark. "This game was a game for all seasons - Winter - Summer - Autumn or Spring, golf always seems to be the game, no matter what the clime. Like all good games, judgement was essential for success - not bad judgement - but good judgement; perseverance in golf played a great part and not only did it develop those qualities of self - reliance, but vigilance and coolness were also absolutely essential".

Speaking of golf in a reminiscent way, Sir Norman said that he found that James 2nd, when he was Duke of York, was sent by the Government to Edinburgh to act as Commissioner of Parliament. He was accompanied by a suite composed largely of noblemen, and in order to while away the hours they played golf. Two noblemen of the suite challenged the then Duke of York to a game for very high stakes. The Duke was allowed to pick his partner from any part of Scotland. The Duke accepted the challenge and chose as his partner a local character who played in the name of John Patterson, following the occupation of a shoemaker. The Duke and his partner won easily, and like a Duke, he gave half of the stakes to the local cobbler. If any of those present visited Edinburgh, Sir Norman advised them to go to see the historical monument, No.77 Cannongate, which house was built by the local cobbler with a portion of the stakes which he won when playing with the Duke of York of England. There was also a charge (one of many) brought against Mary, Queen of

Scots, for playing golf too soon after her husband's death. He also found still earlier records, and between the years 1450 and 1500 A.D. golf had taken such a hold upon the people that the Lord's Spiritual and Temporal issued an edict against the playing of golf during certain months because they found that golf was so universally played, and that the use of the bow and arrow – "as used against our auld enemies of England", was being neglected. A fine of 40 shillings was imposed upon those who broke the law, but eventually the King broke his own ruling by playing a game of golf. Sir Norman did not say if the King was fined or if the rule was withdrawn! He did say, "That it was a clean and healthy sport and expressed a hope that the club would be able to extend their course on the other side of the wood (the Heaton side.)"

It was a long speech, but he continued, "More than half a century ago, I was brought as a boy by my father to see Saltaire. He showed me the church, the model dwellings and other buildings that Sir Titus Salt had erected, and then said to me; "My boy, I want you to remember this;- when you grow up, if success be yours, even in a far less degree than it has been with Sir Titus Salt, I hope you will remember the responsibilities that gain of wealth and the holding of wealth carries with it". There was loud applause at this reminiscence.

"After a lapse of over fifty years," added Sir Norman, "when I walked over these fields and through these woods with a few members of the Council, and as I looked down from the rising ground upon those foundations of Sir Titus, I remembered the words of my father, and I have tried to carry out what I know would have been his wish had he lived to see the day." (there were more loud cheers.) "I am sure," concluded Sir Norman, "that in many ways, and in different ways, hundreds and thousands of people will, as time goes on, be glad that these spaces were saved as open spaces for the people of Shipley. It is now my very great pleasure to formally declare the Course and the Club-House open".

The Members continued to play on the eight holes in the playing fields, and the ten holes on the land given by Sir Norman, until 1928. Plans had been made in 1927 for a new Club House to be built on the site of the eighteenth green, (not Council land) where it would be free from the restriction of the sale of alcohol. Sir Norman, as President, was once again requested to open the new acquisition, but on the opening day, February 25th 1928, he announced that, on the previous day, he had conveyed to the Trustees (the Norman Rae Playing Fields Ltd.) some 41 acres or thereabouts, of land on the Heaton side of the golf course "Which would enable Northcliff Golf Club eventually to have the whole of its eighteen holes on land which will never be taken away from it." "The Trustees," he added, "would wish to see the course used by those he described as people with limited means".

To mark the occasion and to recognise Sir Norman's contribution to the Club's development a large framed photograph of him was commissioned by the Club to be prominently displayed on the premises for all time.

The lease on the playing fields course had still some three years to run and the Shipley Council proposed that the Northcliff Club might like to extend the lease and administrate a Municipal Course of nine holes as agents for the Council, or use the land as an additional nine hole course. Neither suggestion was acceptable and the lease was finally relinquished on December 31st 1929.

The generosity of Sir Norman Rae and the foresight of Councillor Jackson and his fellow Councillors had made possible the formation and the future of a prestigious Club.

CHAPTER SEVEN

Darker days

The year of 1926 was to enter the history books as the year of the General Strike. The West Riding of Yorkshire, the recognised world centre of the wool trade, was particularly hit by the slump and the consequent strikes of the workers employed in industry and transport. There were the almost monotonous reports of well established factories going on "short time" or closing altogether. People spoke in hushed tones of this firm or that, which were household names, ceasing trading, their workforce being thrown on the growing list of unemployed.

There appears to be no record of how Sir Norman Rae's firm, Pickles and Rae, Greenhill Mills, Laisterdyke, fared at this troubled time. Doubtless it would feel the depression which had settled like a cloud over the whole wool industry.

Sir Norman was still a very wealthy man and, as a conscientious and kindly employer, his priority would be to alleviate any unnecessary hardship amongst his employees. At the time of writing this biography, he is still spoken of by the older generation as being remembered as a "good man".

Sir Norman was now over sixty - six years old, still very interested in public affairs and still a public benefactor. His plans for Northcliffe Golf Club were very much to the fore. Long ago at his father's Congregational Chapel he had played the organ, and was still ever ready to

PRINTED & PUBLISHED
ENTIRELY ON THE   -
HIGH SEAS -   -   -

. . A . .

IARY

. . OF THE VOYAGE . .

FROM

Engiand to Australia

BY THE ORIENT LINE

R.M.S.

"Orsova."

Leaving London (Tilbury)
Friday, September 1st, 1911.

Due at Brisbane, Queensland,
Monday, October 16th, 1911.

Souvenir programme of R.M.S. "Orsova" voyage to Australia, 1911.

help others in this capacity. It was through the media of music that he had met his wife, Emily Cass, who sang contralto in the choir at Batley. She was the daughter of Joshua Cass of Mirfield.

Her death in 1927 was a severe blow to Sir Norman. She had been his helpmate and companion for over fifty years, supporting him through his rise in fame and fortune from small beginnings to being an M.P. and his gaining a knighthood. She travelled with him on his world-wide business trips, including three visits to Australia and one to India.

A Batley newspaper reporting her death, noted that she gained prominence on the concert platform and as a soloist of Handel's Messiah. She was a member of Batley Choral Society for many years and a member and patron of the Bradford Festival Choral Society.

Her funeral took place a few days before Christmas 1927. It was a very sad time for her husband and family, and as a public figure, it is likely that he would have been almost overwhelmed by the many messages of sympathy received.

It is poignant to note that she died on the 9th of December, 1926.

It was the thirteenth birthday of her grand-daughter, Marion Jean Woodhead.

CHAPTER EIGHT

The gift of Oakwell Hall

Oakwell Hall, Birstall, was the subject of much public outcry in 1926 when the owners, the Rt. Hon. E.A. Fitzroy M.P.(Speaker in the House of Commons) and Alfred Llewelyn Wheeler Esq. proposed to sell the late Elizabethan house, piecemeal or entirely, to Americans eager to possess anything of such great antiquity. The reason for the sale was given in an edition of the Batley News, Feb. 1926. The following are extracts from the report:-

"Reported negotiations for the sale of relics worth £2,000."

"To enable the payment of the death duties etc, of a member of the Fitzroy family, a late ward in Chancery, negotiations are in progress with a firm of antique dealers for the sale of the beautiful internal fittings of Oakwell Hall, Birstall, which, it is reported may soon be sold and dismantled to satisfy the tastes of relic seekers".....

Prominent among the features of this ancient and interesting mansion are its unique oak panellings and embellishments, which are estimated to be worth at least £2,000 and its latticed windows."

This caused much anxiety concerning the future of the Hall. Suggestions that it might be used as a convalescent home or a golf club were dismissed by the Council as impracticable. The Clerk to the Council, Mr. Horace Grey,

Oakwell Hall, entrance 1976.

Oakwell Hall, rear view 1976.

said that before the war when the Hall had first been for sale, he had advocated its purchase. Since then things had altered, the Council were now faced with much expenditure on account of unemployment, and he could not therefore advise the Council to take the financial responsibility of the purchase.

To allow the Hall, or part of it, to be transported to America was unthinkable, so an appeal was made to local business men to try to raise the £3,000 needed. Sadly, the required sum was not forthcoming.

The Hall was built in 1583 by John Batt (or Batte) on the site of a house previously owned by his father, Henry Batte in 1565 (at that time the appended "e" was used). The house remained in their family for over one hundred and fifty years, and as their fortunes waxed and waned so the house was improved or neglected in accord with their prosperity. The Batt family had a long and chequered history and many tales, wild or otherwise circulate about them. One of them, William, died in mysterious circumstances in 1684, he was "killed in sport - slain by Mr. Gream at Barne near London." The mystery of his death gave rise to the rumour that on the day of his death in London, his ghost had been seen entering his room at Oakwell and leaving behind a bloody footprint. It was said that the mark could not be removed except by cutting out the stained floorboard, which many years later the then owner of Oakwell decided to do.

As it is with any ancient building, the various ownerships led to a variety of usage. Perhaps the most timely one of all was a Mrs. Hannah Cockill who, with her three daughters, ran Oakwell as a boarding school for thirteen young ladies aged between nine and seventeen. This led to Charlotte Brontë's memorable visit, to her absorbing the atmosphere and making Oakwell the role site for "Fieldhead" in her novel "Shirley", thereby endowing Oakwell with a fictional immortality.

A year had gone by from the opening of the fund, during which Sir Norman, saddened at the death of his wife in December 1927, had found support with the old friends of his Batley days, the Taylors. He had become engaged, or was soon to be, to Miss G. Elsie Taylor, a member of Batley Council. Sir Norman had close family connections with the Taylor family. His eldest brother, Charles James Rae who lived in Naples, had married Theodore Taylor's cousin, a Miss Clarkson.

Sir Norman took the initiative to support the Oakwell appeal and was joined by his friend and neighbour at Rossett Green, Mr. John Earl Sharman. He was a Halifax born business man with connections in the Birstall and Bradford areas. Sir Norman said that it was sentiment which had prompted them both to intervene and offer the necessary amount, not only to buy the Hall but to pay for its repair. As they were both travellers and had met Brontë lovers throughout the world, they did not want the Hall to be lost. Sir Norman said, "It seems to me that there is very little in the West Riding still worth preserving. We should grasp every opportunity of saving what remains."

The ancient structure, fine oak panelling and intricate plasterwork was in urgent need of care and restoration. It is interesting to note that while a careful survey was being carried out on the visible structure of the Hall prior to its purchase, an equally important geological one was made of the foundations. The Hall and extensive grounds were situated in a district where there were deep working coal mines, the surveyors would be relieved to learn that the following situations applied to Oakwell :-

"The Middleton Main Seam. A pillar of coal was left for support of Oakwell Hall and buildings when this seam was worked about 1868 to 1870.

Blocking Bed. No workings have taken place in the vicinity or under the Hall or Buildings.

Beeston Bed. Same reply as Blocking Bed.

Black Bed. A pillar of coal was left for the support of the Hall and Buildings when this seam was worked by the Howden Clough Colliery Company between 1922 and 1926." - (History and description of Oakwell Hall and Manor. by J. Sprittler).

If all this seems rather technical, it must have been re-assuring to the layman to know that Oakwell Hall rested on an undisturbed bed of best Yorkshire coal!

It was the friends' intention that the Hall should be given on trust to the Birstall Urban District Council for the enjoyment of the public, and a public meeting was held at Oakwell on the third Jan. 1928 to outline the proposed conditions of the gift.

A report in a Yorkshire paper the following day makes interesting reading :-

"OAKWELL HALL BECOMES PUBLIC PROPERTY."

The conditions upon which Oakwell Hall, Birstall, the Elizabethan house of Brontë association, is to become a gift to the public from Sir H.Norman Rae and Mr. J.E. Sharman of Harrogate, were made public at a meeting yesterday of persons who had subscribed to a fund for public purchase of the Hall. Mr. W. Rhodes, the Chairman of Birstall Urban Council presided. The meeting was held at the Hall and the two donors were present.

It was announced that the Birstall Council had accepted the invitation of the donors to become public trustees of the Hall and that the contract would be signed the following day. As from today therefore, Oakwell Hall is public property, held in trust by the Birstall Council.

On the motion of the Rev. P.J. Shaw (of York), seconded by Mr. Reginald Cooke (of Ben Rhydding), it was decided to hand over to the Council the £700 previously subscribed for the public purchase, to be a nucleus for the fund, the income from which will be devoted to the maintenance and preservation of the Hall and estate. A local appeal for funds is to be made so that, if possible, the care of the estate should not be a charge on local rates.

CONDITIONS OF USE.

Draft conditions, to be embodied in a trust deed, which were approved by the meeting, lay down that the

Hall is to be used only as a specimen for inspection and enjoyment by the public, and for the accommodation and exhibition of domestic furniture of the 17th and 18th and early 19th Centuries, and of pictures and other objects relating to the history and past use of the premises. Private occupation, except by a caretaker, is forbidden. Public access will be allowed subject to reasonable regulations which are to be made and administered by a committee of six members of the Birstall Council and one nominee each of the Yorkshire Archeological Society, the Thoresby Society and the Brontë Society. The Committee will have power to make a charge for admission. The Birstall Council is to maintain the property in a suitable state, and may apply income from subscribed funds for that purpose.

Sir Norman Rae said that Mr. Sharman and he felt it a privilege to make such a gift to the public, and it was a special pleasure to him since the first thirty years of his life had been spent in the neighbouring town of Batley. Oakwell Hall was one of the most beautiful old residences in the West Riding, and the more valuable for its interesting Brontë associations.

BRONTË AUTOGRAPH.

"The very room", Sir Norman continued, "in which they were meeting was referred to in "Shirley", and Charlotte Brontë's autograph on the window in the large hall was acclaimed to be genuine. The West Riding had not many such assets to preserve, and unless they cared for such as remained, the time would soon arrive when there would be little or nothing worth preserving. It would have been a shame if the Hall had been purchased and taken to

America, and they were indebted to the owners of the property who acquainted the public when that possibility arose." Mr. Sharman and he were glad to have had the opportunity of preserving the noble building for their native county and as far as possible intended to have the grounds laid out as an old English garden. The only structural alterations to the Hall would be those necessary for its preservation. He pleaded that the immediately surrounding district should be improved by neighbouring property owners and by the local authority. Mr. Sharman said that no-one wished to see such a fine piece of old architecture leave the country and he was glad to have been associated with Sir Norman in the movement for its retention.

A PUPIL AT THE HALL.

Mr. J. Charlesworth (of Wakefield) and Mr. Percy Robinson (of Leeds) thanked the donors. The latter observed that another fine example of old domestic architecture a few miles away on the other side of Leeds was to be pulled down for removal to Scotland. It would have been disastrous if under similar circumstances Oakwell Hall had been lost to the county. Among those present at the meeting was Mrs. Dixon of York, who, it was mentioned, was a pupil at Oakwell Hall sixty years ago under Miss Carter. Mrs. Dixon is a daughter of the late Mr. John Smith, a former Birstall solicitor and Clerk to the old Birstall Local Board. In her younger days she was aquainted with Miss Ellen Nussey, the confidential friend of Charlotte Brontë.

_____   Yorkshire Post. 4. 1.1928

So it appeared that the Conveyance could go ahead with no problems, but sadly, things did not work out so easily. There had already been a delay, Mr. Wheeler, the joint vendor of Oakwell died on the 27th September 1927, (a Mr. Graham Blunt, solicitor, then acted as trustee of Mr. Wheeler's estate). Then, Mr. John Sharman, who had recently re-married, died in November 1928. He was on his honeymoon at Bournemouth. Regrettably, his death was soon to be followed by that of Sir Norman on the 31st December 1928.

The two men who had hoped to see their dream of Oakwell Hall becoming the safe property of the people did not live to see its finalisation, nor find their own chance of a second happiness.

After these unavoidable delays, it was not until the 6th September 1929, that Sir Norman's son and daughter were able to complete the transaction and ensure that Oakwell Hall was held in Trust by Birstall Urban District Council, for the people, in perpetuity.

Photograph inscribed "Fardie" the children's name for their grandfather, on the lawn at Rossett Green, August 1928. He died four months later.

CHAPTER NINE

Death of Sir Henry Norman Rae

In July 1928, Sir Norman's health was causing his doctor some anxiety. He was suffering from angina.

According to a reference to his illness in The Batley News:-

"It was only six months since his return from America. A breakdown followed and his condition became critical, though only a week or so ago he seemed to be greatly improved, giving rise to hopes of better health".

Sir Norman's death was reported by the same newspaper which gave it prominent headlines in the edition of Saturday, January 5th 1929. Quoting in full, this is how the sad details reached the people of Batley:-

"By the death of Sir H. Norman Rae, formerly M.P. for the Shipley Division of Yorkshire, Batley has lost one of its most distinguished sons, for his father, the late James Rae was pastor of Hanover Street Congregational Church for 31 years, until his retirement in 1885. Sir Norman died suddenly in Batley on Monday afternoon at Westfield House, Healey, the residence of Councillor G. Elsie Taylor, to whom he had recently become engaged.

At 1.45p.m. on Monday he left his residence at Rossett Green, Harrogate, in company with Miss Taylor, and travelled by motor car to Leeds, where he made a business call. The journey was afterwards continued to Westfield

House. Shortly before four o'clock Sir Norman complained of flatulence, and while taking tea his head suddenly drooped. Miss Taylor telephoned for Dr. J.H.Woods, J.P. who found Sir Norman was dying. A few minutes later he passed away. He was last seen by his medical adviser on Dec. 5th, and in view of the facts the West Riding Coroner (Mr. C.J. Haworth) decided that no inquest was necessary".

Reference was made to a memorable speech by Sir Norman at the annual dinner of the Batley Grammar School Old Boys' Association the previous February:-

"His words on that occasion will not easily be forgotten by those who had the pleasure of listening to him. His high ideals in his business and private life may very well be summed up in his own words on that occasion – "There must be something more in all successful careers than the mere making of money," he said, "otherwise life was a failure. The value of what they possessed - money or knowledge - was determined by the use they were able to make of it. Worldy success was a good thing in its way but he considered character was far above it, that success without character seemed to him to be of little or no avail."

At the same dinner, he mentioned once again one of his most treasured possessions, a letter from the late John Bright, the great orator and politician, on the art of public speaking.

Sir Norman's death came as a great shock to all who knew him or knew of him. Tributes came from friends everywhere and in all walks of life. The small local authorities who had benefited most by his unfailing generosity and help, felt bereft. The newspapers of Harrogate, Bradford and Shipley filled columns for his obituary, reminding their readers of Sir Norman's life and achievments. It made impressive reading, from his birth at Prospect House, Healey, to his death at Westfield House, Healey. Strangely it was but a stone's throw from where he was born.

Many were the tributes paid to Sir Norman. One from Mr. J. Balmforth, presiding at Harrogate Police Court, referred to the death of Sir Norman, "Whose public life," he said, "was an example to younger people." Councillor C.B. Carter, a close personal friend, said that "The country as well as Yorkshire, had lost one of its outstanding figures, and a shrewd business man. The social life of the West Riding would suffer a great loss. Sir Norman was a man of sterling qualities."

He was described as "Kindly and modest, yet impatient of second-rate effort in any service or cause. His speeches were characterised by directness and brevity, and his will was exceptionally tenacious. He never forgot a kindness and was extremely loyal to friends, who in turn, had a strong admiration for the fine integrity and manly characteristics which lay behind his businesslike exterior."

In Shipley, his Constituency when he was a Member of Parliament, there was much sadness. The local people had come to love and respect him. He had done so much for the small town, as was recalled at the Shipley Urban District Council on the 29th. January 1929. The Council minutes for that date read:-

"Before commencing the ordinary business of the meeting, the Chairman, Councillor Victor Waddilove, referred to the death of Sir Norman H. Rae, which had occurred on the 31st December 1928.

Sir Norman had occupied an important position in the business community. He had represented the Shipley Division in Parliament, and it was largely due to his efforts that the Bradford Extension Bill was defeated on the Second Reading. The Chairman also referred to Sir Norman's generosity in presenting to the town the Northcliffe Woods and Playing Fields, and said that he considered Sir Norman was the greatest benefactor to the Shipley District since the time of the late Sir Titus Salt. He proposed that a letter of condolence be sent to the family.

Councillor Cowgill seconded the resolution, and the members signified their concurrence by rising in their places."

Sir Norman had left explicit instructions for the conducting of his funeral. In a letter to his executors he stated:-

"I wish my funeral to be of great simplicity. Instead of the burial service, I wish the following passages of the Bible to be read with reverence and beauty - Luke, chapter 24, verses 13 - 32."

"I also wish two hymns to be sung by a soprano or contralto voice, - Abide with me - verses 1,2,4,7,and 8, and O Lord of Heaven and Earth and Sea, from the Scots Presbyterian Church Hymnary.

I have lived my life with a thankful heart to my Creator and I commend a spirit of thankfulness to my family and friends. I have enjoyed my life and have tried, though with many imperfections, to do my duty and play the game".

The service which, (with the addition of the 23rd Psalm) was as he had wished, "of great simplicity". It was conducted by the Rev. J.W. Lightley, President of the Wesleyan Conference, who paid tribute to Sir Norman "for his many kindly deeds - the manifestation of unselfishness and a kindly spirit which looked not upon his own needs but upon the needs of others."

His funeral took place at Harlow Cemetery, Harrogate, on Thursday the 3rd of January 1929. While the cortege passed by, motorists stopped their cars and stood, bareheaded. Pedestrians who had known Sir Norman personally or by his philanthropic reputation, halted to pay their last tributes. A road sweeper, his head bared and bent in respect, illustrated the esteem in which Sir Norman was held among all classes.

His grave at Harlow Cemetery lies near the small side gate, overhung with the branches of an old chestnut tree.

HENRY NORMAN RAE KNIGHT
1860 - 1928
He was "A gentle man."

—————

The grave of Sir H. Norman Rae, Harlow Cemetery, Harrogate.

In Loving Memory of
EMILY,
WIFE OF H. NORMAN RAE.
DIED DEC. 9TH 1927. AGED 68.

ALSO OF
H. NORMAN RAE, KNIGHT.
D DEC. 31ST 1928. AGED 66.
AND OF THEIR DAUGHTER,

CASSIE,
WOODHEAD. DIED 14TH JUNE 1951. AGED 66.
ALSO OF
ARTHUR WOODHEAD,
ED 3RD MAY 1963. AGED 77.

The grave of Sir H. Norman Rae, Harlow Cemetery, Harrogate.

In Memoriam.

✠

Henry Norman Rae,
Knight.

Died
31st December, 1928.

Aged 68 Years.

✠

Order of service. Funeral, Sir H. N. Rae.

CHAPTER TEN

"Update"

Although Sir Norman's life ended on the 31st December. 1928, the gifts which he made to the people are still appreciated and cared for by the younger generation. There have been changes - time and circumstance have necessitated such, but mainly they conform to the wishes and hopes that were Sir Norman's at the time of giving.

The last gift, that of Oakwell Hall, has become the beautiful place which he and Mr. Sharman envisaged, well cared for and much visited. Dating from the time of Elizabeth 1st. it is a treasure house of West Riding history and architecture. Though the original Birstall Council now forms part of the larger Kirklees Metropolitan Council (the present trustees) the conditions of the original Trust are still adhered to:- that the Hall "be used only as a specimen for inspection and enjoyment by the public, and for the accommodation and exhibition of domestic furniture of the 17th 18th and early 19th Centuries, and of pictures and other objects relating to the history and past use of the premises". A further benefit has been the formation of a Country Park at Oakwell, thus fulfilling Sir Norman's plea that the immediate surrounding district should be improved.

The Norman Rae Nursing Home was the birthplace of thousands of Shipley children. It is not unusual to hear elderly people proudly declare that they were one of Norman Rae's 'babies', as often were their children and grandchildren! The large sign facing Bradford Road prominently displayed the name, "THE NORMAN RAE NURSING HOME" to be read by all who passed by, but sometime in the 1980's it was removed and the sign SHIPLEY HOSPITAL erected. The usage had changed from maternity care to one of a more general small hospital but the care and kindness remained the same. Many people still had cause to be grateful for its services, not least in that it was local for Shipley's inhabitants.

The hospital was closed again in 1994-5 for complete renovation and extension. It was re-opened on 4th September 1996, seventy three years to the day after its first opening by H.R.H. Princess Mary. It was to be a re-habilitation centre for people who had been in hospital in Bradford but were still in need of greater support than was available in their own homes. Beautifully refurbished, it was described as "The jewel in the crown" of the Bradford Community Health Service when it was formally re-opened by Sir Norman's grandson, Mr. Norman Woodhead. In his speech at the opening, Mr. Woodhead remarked, "I know how delighted my grandfather would have been to see how his nursing home has been improved to set up a new Shipley Hospital. He was always concerned with the well being of his fellow men. This is a very special moment because this building means a lot to our family. It is really beautiful".

It was a very proud moment too for all the people who attended the ceremony.

Shipley had, once again, got its very own hospital!

———————————

Mr Norman Woodhead. Grandson of Sir Norman Rae.
Picture courtesy of Telegraph and Argus, Bradford.

The Norman Rae Scholarships have enabled many boys and girls to enter a university. The first scholarship was awarded to Eveleen Lyles at the Hanson Secondary School. She was to study for the medical profession. The second scholarship went to Elma V. Nowell at the Grange Road Secondary School. This was in September 1918.

That there were many more scholarships awarded throughout the years is certain, but tracing the recipients has proved a daunting task. That is, until one day quite recently, when the author was chatting to an old acquaintance, Mrs. Janet Oldfield, who 'just happened' to have been a Norman Rae Scholarship winner in the early 1960's! She attended Belle Vue Girls' High school at the time.

It is difficult to discover if the awards are still being made, or what has happened to the investments which made the awards possible. No doubt that there will be many more people who can proudly say, "I too won a Norman Rae Scholarship".

To record all the events which have taken place in Northcliffe since its opening in 1920 would require a book in itself. Sir Norman may have witnessed a partial realisation of his dream to make a living and growing space for the people before his death in 1928, but it was from the years 1930 - 1940 and onwards that the fields and woods of Northcliffe were of immeasurable value to Shipley people.

The fields were to be the site of many a Shipley Gala, held when times were grim and there was little cheer to be had. People flocked together to applaud the local beauties elected to be Gala Queen and her attendants, the comic bands, and the wonderfully decorated trade floats. It mattered not that the Gala of one year differed little from that of the year before. The faces and costumes were fresh and new, even if the routine was much the same. The Fire Service would put its men through their drill at breakneck speed, the Police dogs would apprehend the burglar who was suitable identified by his convict costume, and the gymnastic teams displayed their skill building living pyramids of supple young men, the crowds holding their collective breath as the final slender young man climbed to form the apex.

During the lean years of war the 'Holidays at Home' week gave some semblance of carefree festivity to folk who were restricted in travel and holidays. Each day found something fresh to watch, and for the children it was a week of delight. Never mind if some days brought rain, there was always the next day to look forward to, and the anticipation of next year's 'Holidays at Home'.

The post - war years saw Northcliffe struggling to regain its pre - war appearance. The handsome shelters, because of restrictions on money available for repairs, were deemed unsafe and were eventually demolished. The stretches of land which had been ploughed to grow food crops were once more sown with grass. Skilled gardeners and woodsmen returned from the forces and began their battle with nature to make Northcliffe bloom again, and to draw gasps of appreciation at the splendour of the flower - beds.

Northcliffe had survived and in doing so had been the means of helping Shipley feel alive again. Nowadays it needs people again to tend it carefully. Some trees require expert attention if the life of the wood is to be extended, and there are young saplings to be planted to be the nucleus of the future woodland.

Northcliffe is a treasure which needs constant guarding.

The firm of Pickles and Rae was sold and all connections with the family discontinued. The building had many occupiers until it was purchased by the Bradford Woolcombers Association. It now is no longer a working mill, but a complex of small firms, reflecting that wool is now not the trade that it used to be in Bradford or the West Riding of Yorkshire.

BIBLIOGRAPHY

Newspapers........ The Yorkshire Observer.
                   The Shipley Times and Express.
                   Shipley Guardian.
                   The Harrogate Herald.
                   The Batley News.
                   The Batley Reporter.

Libraries.......... Harrogate.
                   Shipley.
                   Bradford Reference, and
                   Bradford Archives.
                   Leeds Reference.
                   Laurencekirk and Stonehaven.
                   Batley.

Books.............. Shipley Council Minutes.
                   The History of Shipley.
                                 Alfred Cousin.
                   The History of Congregationalism.
                                 J.G.Miall.
                   The History of Batley Grammar School.
                   Northcliffe Golf Club.
                                 R.Hodgkinson.
                   The History of Batley.
                                 J. Fearnsides.
                   The rise and progress of Batley.
                                 Jas. Williams.
                   The first century of Silcoates School.
                                 H.Hislop Oakley
                   The History of the Parish and
                   Burgh of Laurencekirk.
                                 W.R.Fraser.